FISHING
the
Cape Cod
Canal

D. J. Muller

Burford Books

Printed in the United States of America.

10 9 8 7 6 5 4 3 2 1

Library of Congress Cataloging-in-Publication Data
is on file with the Library of Congress.

Contents

ACKNOWLEDGMENTS

You cannot write a book without lots of help. Trust me this is my fourth book and it is the good people that I have made friends with along the way that give you, the reader, a good final product. I have traveled all over the striper universe. I have seen a lot of striper terrain and I have caught a lot of bass, but more important than the fish are the people I have met along the way. Their kindness gives my experiences length, enjoyment, and validity.

I want to thank my brothers that I work alongside, fish with, and interact with all year long. They are great to bounce things off of with their experience and work ethic. Pat, Koz, Victor, Lanyard, Beater, Jolliffe, Andrew, and my main man, Murty.

I want to sincerely thank the following good people for helping my get this book complete!

Tom Cootz (Red Top Bait and Tackle) and Jeff Miller (Canal Bait and Tackle), two great guys that take their businesses seriously and have a vested interest is seeing guys fishing the Canal do it right and do it safely. Bob "the Bull" a.k.a. The Rocketman. Tony Orlando, a great fisherman and a great person. Ron McKee and Lee Boullie from Striper Maine-iac, (the two headed monster from Maine!). Stanley Darmofalski, great insights! Ryan Collins (myfishingcapecod.com), great stuff, good reading, good viewing. Derek Lindquist and Ryan Fontaine, knowledgeable and great (funny) stories. Wayne and Peter Hess, the makers of the best pencil popper in the world—Guppy. Dave Anderson. Walter Morris, Wally Custom Lures, the world's best secret. Don Guimelli, the best plugbuilder of our time! John Doble at johndoblephoto graphy.com, check out his great work! Jamie Hawley, Flatlander Surfcasting, best bag builder alive. Of course my chiropractor, Dr. Barbara Costas at Sea Coast Chiropractic in Pt. Pleasant Beach, NJ. My "life saver"!

I would be remiss if I didn't mention my two Canal buddies Evan and Scott Clough.

An extra big thank you to Tony Navarro—he has passion for the Ditch. Thanks for your great ideas brother!

Big Dave Thomashey, super guy, incredible Canal knowledge base and a pleasure to deal with. Thank you buddy for all your help!

All my love to Jenn and the Nut!

PREFACE

I feel the need to mention a couple things about the writing of this book. First is that I wrote it with the word "respect" in mind. I respect those who fish the Canal regularly and/or call it their home water. Thus I went out of my way not to burn spots or get too specific about places to fish. I made sure that I emphasized respect for the Ditch, the parking, and those who do call it home. As I do with all of my writings and teachings, I leave a lot of room for the reader to learn and develop on his or her own. In many areas I have left it up to you to figure it out for yourself. I will lead you to the water, but now it's up to you to drink. I did that because the Canal is so multifaceted, so complex, with so many options, that I could never give anyone that much detail and also because people are different and tend to like different things.

As I grew and developed as a fisherman on the Canal, I was always asking questions and trying to hone my skills sets or learn something new to give me a little better edge. I remember on one particular trip I happened to run across three guys that I consider Canal sharpies. I was fortunate enough to spend some quality time with all three, and I asked questions—the best way to fish the Canal, the best places to fish, the best lures, you get the idea. Each guy gave me a very different answer from the others, it truly amazed me. I realized that there are no black-and-white answers here.

I know the question will come about, "What qualifies you to write this book?" Besides the fact that I am a writer and I am capable, my answer is this: I have talked to many, many guys that fish the Ditch regularly, every day. Many of them are locked in on specific and favored techniques and specific spots, and so on. You talk to another guy and you get an entirely different version about his techniques and places that are best. So as someone who doesn't fish it every day, and someone who stands back and looks at the big picture, someone who is objective and collects multiple opinions, I can actually see the forest for the trees. I can report objectively and I believe that is fair.

Lastly I want to point out that I do not mention brands of rods and reels specifically because the technology changes so fast. Based on the fact that this book is a guide for those looking to familiarize themselves with or introduce themselves to the Canal, by the time they roll up their sleeves, do some fishing, hit some online forums and talk to some of the local shops, they should have a good idea on what they will need to buy for themselves.

So dig in, enjoy, and may your time spent fishing the Ditch be productive!

D. J. Muller
March, 2017

INTRODUCTION

I am an avid surfcaster and I love to travel near and far in search of striped bass. I have had the good fortune of fishing places that people can only dream of. Big bass and endless sunsets, that's what makes me happiest.

I have been fishing the Canal for about fifteen years and while I would never classify myself as a Canal sharpie or anything close to that, I can certainly hold my own. I have had some very good sessions there and had very good success. I have made the commitment to dive head-first into its fishery and have found, as many have, a place of comfort and a great source of contentment and gratification from fishing its banks. Being the author of three prior books, I noticed that there was a void in the "guide" department, so I decided it was important to write a book for those that are either new to the Canal or coming from a distance to fish it. It will surely also help those that have been fishing it for a while and those looking for a foothold in moving forward. I hope you will find this book comprehensive and informative. I had input from very experienced local fishermen in writing it, for which I am forever grateful, and I believe the reader will be, too!

You grab your rod and coffee and slam the door to your truck. Off you go into the early morning darkness. You didn't sleep a wink last night. You park and dress and down a gravel incline, through a tree covered path, you shuffle down another dirt hill and you come to the asphalt path. You look hard into the darkness and you see your spot is unoccupied, so your heart is happy. Soon the sky will run to purple and then orange, and hopefully a good push of big stripers will chase a hot school of mackerel right past you. The fast-pulling currents of the Big Ditch will be your partner for the next couple of hours and your trusted rod and your favorite lures will be your gateway to what you hope is a great striper.

The morning started out very quiet, actually much quieter than usual, bordering on disappointing. It was 8:30 AM and I only had a couple of small bass to show for my effort. I rounded up my group of friends and we went over the details of the morning. All reports were like a broken record: "Yeah a couple shorts that was it." My buddies and I had been out since 4:30 AM and a big hot breakfast seemed to be calling from a distant Leo's Breakfast Restaurant. It was at that point where something caught my attention from out of the corner of my eye. There was a massive explosion on the surface of water. "What do we have here?" I asked. All heads turned. Then I noticed another blow-up further upstream. They were moving our way. "Let's give it another 20!" I said. Without a second thought everyone scrabbled for a perch on the rocks below.

When I talk about what happened next, the best description of the morning was that King Neptune opened the cage at the bottom of the Canal and let the titans out! For the next 40 minutes all hell broke loose. My first bass was a low-40. Then Muller-luck kicked in right on time. As I wrestled with the 40, I stuck my rod down into the rocks standing it straight up as I unhooked and released the great fish. After watching my fish swim away I grabbed my rod and pulled it, instead of carefully lifting it, and I broke it about fifteen inches above the butt. I don't know if you have ever fished with a rod with a broken butt, but I did and it is almost impossible to reel in a lure, let alone a big fish. So after seriously struggling with another big bass I had to go with my back-up rod which I would never normally use in the Ditch but I brought it along for my short game, fishing tight to the edge—I had no other option. (It was a Century Stealth S-1. It is probably my favorite rod but certainly not a Canal rod.) I had no choice—things were going crazy and the bass were big.

So here we go with my luck again, I cast out and the biggest, bruiser bass hit my pencil popper and off she went. Thankfully it was late morning and the crowd had all but disappeared. I'm going to shorten a long story, I couldn't stop the fish and I didn't gain one inch on that fish for ten minutes. I just held on and waited it out, I was going to wear her down and then do what I had to do. At about the halfway point I began to gain, one inch at a time. She had set up in a rip down from me about 70 yards. I decided, which I never do, to walk down to the fish. I worked my way down stumbling and bumbling on the rip-rap all the way. I was gaining line and I was getting more and more pumped (like I needed more pumping up) to see this fish and I was seriously starting to question the holding power of my Guppy pencil and all things connecting it to me. I honestly didn't think that I was going to land this fish and I prepared myself for a major letdown, a breakoff or a pulled hook or something of the sort. It was now close to 20 minutes in and I was getting her, I saw her come up as I applied great pressure against her and the current. The huge dorsal fin broke the surface and I almost . . . well you know. I reeled down and pulled up until I had my leader in my hand and I dragged a huge, tired cow to my feet, I was completely whooped myself as you can imagine. There she lay, a bass to close to 50 pounds. I have had some 50-pound bass in my day and this one was right there.

I looked around for one of my pals but none was in sight. I saw a father and son duo, (who have since become friends) fishing bait up on the rocks, and I asked the kid to take some pictures for me. Evan accommodated willingly and was real good about doing it. He was awed by the fish, as was I! It was his first day striper fishing. I then took the fish and began to walk into the water. "Hey what are you doing?" he asked. "I'm releasing her." "Why?" he asked. "It's because it's what I do. I want to have more of these fish in the future. If we kill them all there won't be any future for these fish. They have to be allowed to reproduce."

He understood. I held the fish, nose into the current and I just held her there with my hand on her bottom jaw, and my thumb in her mouth. Her life-less tail swung in the current. I patiently stayed with her. Strangely at one point a walker passing by yelled down to me, "It's about time someone let one of those fish go!" Finally, after about ten minutes the great fish showed some life biting down on my thumb. Not yet, I thought—I wanted to sure that she had the rest she needed to go and be safe. After another

Big Sweetheart. This good fish came well after sunrise and after the water was pulling hard and fast. After a 20-minute battle, the fish was released to reproduce and to fight another day.

minute or so, she put up her greatest resistance and I knew she was ready to go. I opened my hand and she was free. Slowly she kicked that broom tail and moved slowly away, healthy and straight as she disappeared into the waters from which she came. What an outstanding feeling. Monster came, monster left. There is no way I could ask for more. The beauty of the Canal!

CHAPTER 1

GETTING STARTED

UNDERSTANDING THE CAPE COD CANAL

The Cape Cod Canal is seven miles long, 480-feet wide and approximately 32 feet deep. For the surfcaster it is one of the most fascinating and compelling places to fish for striped bass on the East Coast, a fishery unique unto itself. Whether you are the most seasoned surfcaster or if you are totally new to the game, there is something there for you. The fast waters of the Canal give multiple options on multiple levels. From the "daytimer" who just wants to go out and make a few casts on an early-June day and enjoy the sun and hopefully pull a "keepah," to the guy who does it every night working the night tides and shadow lines with monster bass in the balance. Two features of the Canal, besides the fishing, help draw people to its banks. One is the service road that runs both sides of the waterway, which gives you the chance to move around with ease, walking or riding a bike along a seven mile stretch of superb water on each side. Second is that there are plenty of access points and enough parking so fishermen can spread out and find fish, especially when the fishing gets good and the crowds get crazy. (On a side note, please respect the neighborhood parking—if it says it is a four-car spot, then it is a four car spot. There are other places to park. And please come and go quietly, especially during off hours.)

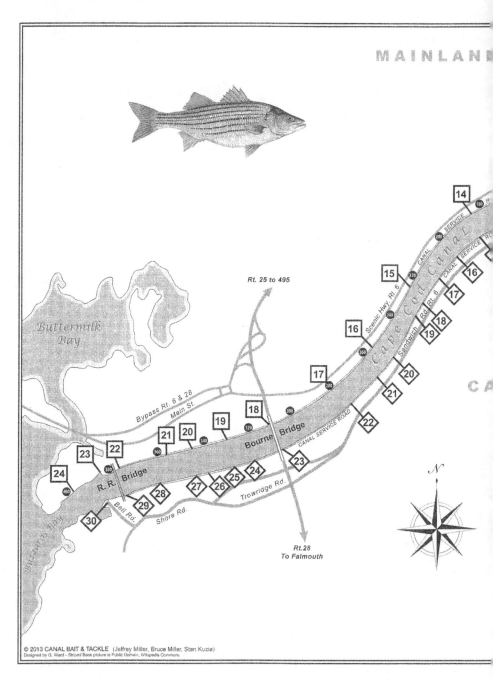

So what is it that makes the Big Ditch so productive and so compelling?
In short: it's a funnel, through which everything must pass.
Map courtesy Canal Bait & Tackle.

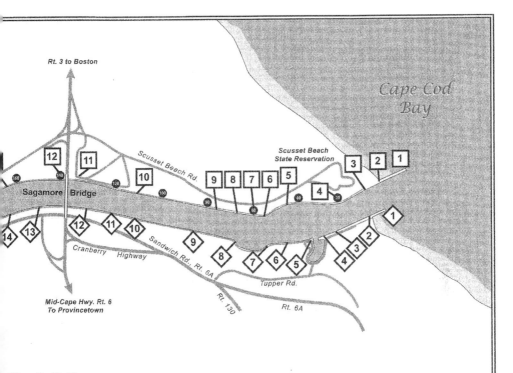

Rt. 3 to Boston

Cape Cod Bay

Scusset Beach Rd.

Scusset Beach
State Reservation

12 11

160 140

Sagamore Bridge

120

10

100

9 8 7 6 5

80

60

3 2 1

4

40 20

14 13

12 11 10

Cranberry Highway

Sandwich Rd., Rt. 6A

9

8

7 6 5

1

2

3

4

Mid-Cape Hwy. Rt. 6
To Provincetown

Rt. 130

Tupper Rd.

Rt. 6A

E COD

◇ Cape Side from East - West

1. Sandwich Jetty
2. Murphy's Beach
3. Joe's Lobster
4. Bulkhead
5. Harrys Corner
6. Iron Works
7. Apple Tree
8. Paddy Gibbons
9. Sagamore Inn
10. Freighthouse
11. Engineers Building
12. Post Office
13. The Pipe
14. Portugee Hole
15. Stone Bay's
16. Overlook
17. Split Rock
18. Double Rip Rap
19. Midway Gate
20. Old Radar
21. Jungle
22. Sandbank (Ice Arena)
23. Rec Hole
24. Trowbridge
25. Keene Sreet
26. Lobster Pound
27. Aptuxet
28. Worcester Surfcasters
29. Railroad Bridge Hole
30. Bell Road

□ Mainland Side from East - West

1. Scusset Jetty
2. Breakwater
3. Pip's Rip
4. Good Hole/Pole 20
5. Dolphins
6. Murderers Row
7. Mudbank
8. Fish Pier
9. Scusset Creek
10. Stone Church
11. Friendly's Parking Lot
12. Sagamore West
13. Muscle Bed
14. Herring Run
15. Cribbin
16. 100 Stairs
17. Pole 280
18. Bourne North
19. Old Bridge
20. Play Land
21. Coal Yard
22. Fisherman Statue
23. Army Corp
24. Mass Maritime

The Canal connects two huge bodies of water, Buzzards Bay to the south and west and Cape Cod Bay to the north and east. Fish moving from south to north or north to south have to pass through this relatively tight area. Fish travel either through the Canal or out and around, east of the Elizabeth Islands, around Martha's Vineyard and Nantucket and then out around Cape Cod. Since its opening in 1914, the Canal has become a shortcut for navigation. Boats navigating along the east coast use it as a more direct line to points north without going out and around Cape Cod. Fish use it in much the same way, as they instinctively push north and south during migration periods. Everything that swims in the Atlantic Ocean passes through the Canal at some point—whales, bluefin tuna, seals, dolphin, and sunfish have all been spotted in the Canal. There was even a sailfish caught in the Ditch in 2013—check it out on You Tube.

The baitfish travel the same path, making for a dynamic set-up whenever predator and prey collide here. On certain tides, at certain times of the year, striped bass push huge shoals of bait through the Canal, using the Ditch like a funnel to their advantage. When this happens it allows the surfcaster a great chance to catch stripers, and lots of them, in a short period of time. At other times, under more normal conditions, the bass continue use the fast-moving waters to their advantage. As bait moves through the Canal's turbid waters the bass have the upper hand because they have no problem navigating the hard current, being much larger and stronger than the baitfish prey. This situation allows for opportunistic feeding and the stripers will congregate and hold in concentrated areas to feed.

Normally the powerful tides of the Canal switch four times a day, although occasionally it may be three. When the tide runs towards the east, or towards Cape Cod Bay, it is simply called the "east" tide, and when it runs west towards Buzzard's Bay, it is called, you guessed it, the "west" tide. There are no conventional incoming or outgoing tides here. The west tide is the dropping or ebb tide and the east tide is the flood. The Canal does not have a universal high tide or a universal low tide; the tides vary at various locations along the seven-mile span. As an example, if high tide on the west-end entrance is at 6:00 AM, then the east end will be high at approximately 8:00 AM. It is important to keep this difference in mind. Another important tide-related time is what time the tide slacks or turns, that is, when it comes to a complete stop then begins to move in the opposite direction. In places like the Canal the tide does not sit still for very long. It will begin to slow about 45 minutes before the switch, slow down to dead, and then sit for approximately 15–20 minutes before it begins to move in the opposite direction.

Reading the Tide Chart

All good surfcasters know their tides and wind directions. One thing that you will come to rely on heavily is the tide chart. After spending some time fishing the Canal you will soon realize that you will have preferred tides, and you will need to know how to read the chart so we will go over this carefully. The Army Corps of Engineers chart, reproduced here, is universally used.

The center column, in bold print, obviously gives us the month and year. The far left column, "Railroad Bridge Current Turns . . .", is what is called breaking tides which is when the tide slacks or comes to a complete stop, and then slowly begins to move in the opposite direction. This chart gives you the time at the Railroad Bridge.

So for example on May 1 the slack tide will begin to move at the Railroad Bridge at 2:36 AM. It is at this time that the tide will begin moving east. It will happen again at 14:54 or 2:54 PM. At 8:54 AM it will turn and go west, which will also happen at 21:12 (9:12 PM in non-military time).

TIDE TABLES

U.S. Army Corps of Engineers
Cape Cod Canal

RAILROAD BRIDGE CURRENT TURNS				MAY 2015		WINGS NECK				R.R. BRIDGE				SANDWICH			
EAST		WEST				HIGH		LOW		HIGH		LOW		HIGH		LOW	
AM	PM	AM	PM			AM	PM	AM	PM	AM	PM	AM	PM	AM	PM	AM	PM
0236	1454	0854	2112	Friday	1	0659	1917	0141	1222	0823	2034	0259	1508	1016	2233	0401	1618
0318	1536	0936	2154	Saturday	2	0736	1953	0102	1249	0859	2111	0343	1550	1059	2313	0445	1701
0400	1612	1012	2230	Sunday	3	0814	2031	0127	1323	0936	2148	0425	1627	1140	2353	0529	1743
0436	1648	1054	2306	Monday	4	0854	2112	0202	1401	1013	2225	0502	1529	----	1222	0611*	1825
0512	1730	1136	2342	Tuesday	5	0936	2154	0244	1445	1048	2301	0536	1608	0033	1303	0654*	1907
0548	1806	----	1218	Wednesday	6	1020	2238	0327*	1531*	1125	2339	0610	1643	0113	1344	0737*	1950
0630	1854	0024	1300	Thursday	7	1105	2325	0409*	1616*	----	1204	0702	1718	0154	1428	0821*	2034
0712	1942	0112	1354	Friday	8	1156	----	0451*	1701*	0021	1250	0814	1758	0239	1515	0907*	2122
0806	2036	0200	1448	Saturday	9	0018	1253	0537*	1752	0110	1342	0911	2128	0327	1606	0956*	2214
0900	2136	0254	1542	Sunday	10	0116	1351	0632	1857	0204	1438	1001	2224	0420	1659	1048*	2309
1006	2236	0354	1636	Monday	11	0215	1448	0741	2014	0300	1534	1052	2322	0516	1756	1143*	----
1106	2342	0454	1736	Tuesday	12	0312	1547	0848	2126	0359	1638	1147	----	0616	1854	0008	1240*
----	1206	0600	1836	Wednesday	13	0413	1650	0950	2242	0508	1749	0021	1240*	0719	1953	0109	1337*

Now look at high water at the Railroad Bridge for May 1, AM tide, it reads 0823 or 8:23 AM is high. Remember that the east tide is the flood. Now look at the Sandwich AM high tide it reads, 1016 or 10:16 AM. What this tells you is that there is approximately a two-hour difference in tides from one end of the Canal to the other. It is safe to assume that if the Railroad Bridge goes slack at 2:36 AM on May 1, that it will slack on the Scusset or Sandwich Jetty on the east end at roughly one hour and forty-five minutes later.

Water Movement

One of the keys to fishing the Cape Cod Canal is to understand current or water flow and speed. The currents of the Canal pull at an average of about four knots or better, and that is a pretty strong current! When they are really pulling on a moon tide it is much faster. Striped bass feed based on current and flow. The faster the water moves, the more they like it.

Understanding water movements helps you to fish smart. Brian Benson took this 50-pound bass from the fast currents of the Ditch. (www.johndoblephotography.com)

The bait for the most part travels against the tide, while the bass travel with the tide and current. There will be times when a school of hunting, feeding bass will come across a big school of bait and then it gets interesting! Predator verses prey, the bass want to pin the bait to where it has nowhere to go. There will be times when you see bait jumping up onto the rocks of the Canal in an attempt to escape. This is what is known as a "blitz," an all-out feeding frenzy. The stripers go on a rampage, as if a switch has been flipped and they will eat just about anything that moves. It makes for great fishing, or in this case, catching!

The consensus largely agrees that morning tides that turn east at first light are great target tides to try to fish. Although I strongly agree with this, I would not limit myself to just those tides. Many

On occasion you will see something like this. This is what happens when a school of bass comes across a school of bait tight to the rocks. Chaos ensues and allows for some great fishing!

times I have gone down to the banks in the late morning, afternoon, or evening and caught fish, simply because I was there and
fishing. To my point, a buddy of mine, Stanley, who has been
fishing the Canal for more than 20 years, emphasized to me that he
has caught more big fish, 40-pound plus, between the hours of 12
and 5 PM. That is an eye-opener.

I don't always need to hit a massive fish to make me happy. Don't fall
into the trap of making a lot of rules for yourself. Please remember
to simply fish, and don't overthink this process—enjoy the situation.
As you experience, learn, and gain confidence you will begin to see
what tides and conditions will work best for you. Be patient, work
hard. You will then begin to stretch yourself, learning more techniques and exploring the more advanced fishing that the Canal offers.

When things get wild and the bass push the bait up against the bank, it is
not unusual to find bait like this mackerel washed up in the rocks.

Migration

Now let's look at some other important factors that will help you better understand fishing the Canal. A key to fishing the Canal is understanding what migration is and how it affects the fishing. Twice a year everything in the striped bass world migrates. In the spring, striped bass, and the bait along with them, travel north from the warm winter confines to the summer grounds of New England. Large populations of striped bass migrate primarily from the Outer Banks of North Carolina and the Chesapeake Bay. In the fall the opposite happens, as all the fish migrate back south. When fish migrate they naturally expend a lot of energy as they travel. Bass can travel up to 12 miles a day while migrating, so the need for food increases greatly. Throw in the need to fatten up and you have heightened periods of feeding, where bass need to consume large amounts of bait.

As a soft rule, two target months for the Canal migration push would be June and September. But remember that in the striper world anything can happen at any time. During migration periods everything gets ratchetted up as large numbers of bass begin to push large schools of bait, such as menhaden (aka bunker or pogies), herring, squid, and mackerel through the funnel of the Ditch, making for great fish-catching opportunities. In late spring and early summer, large bodies of bait and bass alike build up in Buzzards Bay over several weeks as they arrive from the south, and at some point the bass will begin to push these schools of bait through the Canal, leading to huge feeding frenzies. The bait includes just about everything on the stripers menu. When the stripers put on the migration "feedbag," the fishing can get down-right spectacular!

Non-Migration Fishing

While the migration gives you heightened periods of really good fishing, do not be fooled into thinking that these are the only times that you can fish the Canal. The striped bass season in the Canal starts in late May and runs until mid-October. One of the beautiful things about fishing the Canal is that at just about any time during the season, you can go down and pop a sweetheart. I personally have caught some really nice bass in the Ditch in July and August. One late-morning in August I tied into a bass that I never stopped, it just kept going and going. It had to be big. A few casts later I landed a moose that weighed 37 pounds in relatively short order, making me wonder just how big the one that I didn't stop weighed. I have also gone down to relax and throw poppers in the late afternoon with no one around, no pressure, and took some decent bass. Remember if you work hard, the Canal is one of those places where you can be rewarded for effort.

Beautiful striped bass are always available in the Cape Cod Canal. Learning how to extract them can be challenging and extremely gratifying.

The Herring Run

You cannot write a book about fishing the Cape Cod Canal without mentioning the Herring Run—they even named a hotel after it, so it must be important. The Herring Run adds a very interesting feature to the Canal and I don't believe its impact is completely understood by most. The Herring Run Recreational Area is located on Route 6 in Bourne and it is a roadside park, located at about the middle of the Canal on the Mainland side. It is a place where a lot of anglers seem to congregate. The main attraction is the Bournedale Herring Run, which is where Great Herring Pond connects to the Cape Cod Canal. Each year starting in April, river herring or Blueback herring migrate from the ocean, through the Canal, and enter the run at Bournedale, where they swim up the fish ladders on their way to Great Herring Pond, where they lay and fertilize their eggs. They have done this run for many generations. Each year the fry will always return to the river where they

The mouth of the Herring Run seems so calm and peaceful but when the herring drop out of the run it is mayhem! It provides colossal fishing for those in attendance.

were born. Once the adults lay their eggs they will drop back out into the Canal and off they go. In late summer the fry will then be big enough and will also drop out into the Canal.

The herring, like the striped bass, is anadromous, which means they spend the majority of their lives in saltwater and they spawn in fresh water. The herring are a forage base for many marine species, mammals, and birds, making them an important link in the ecosystem as a food base. The herring themselves feed on zooplankton. In very simple terms, as the herring drop out of the herring run in an attempt to make their way back to the ocean, guess who is waiting at the mouth of the run? You got it, stripers, the opportunists! And who waits for the stripers? Yes twenty thousand rod-wielding surfcasters all geared up for what some call fun. But this certainly isn't my kind of fun—I was never into the shoulder-to-shoulder chaos. This situation becomes a circus and should probably be avoided.

This is one of the small holding ponds in the run. At certain times of the year these are chock-full of river herring.

After you are done reading this book you will no longer need to go such a drastic place because you will understand things so much clearer and realize that standing at the mouth of the run is not necessary for catching stripers.

The fish ladders that lead to Great Herring Pond allow the herring to instinctively "run" back and forth between the two bodies of water.

Techniques for Fishing the Ditch

We will be covering a lot of technical stuff later on in the book but for the purpose of overview, I break down the fishing into three categories: the casting of artificials other than jigs or bucktails, fishing bait (which includes eels), and jigging. The casting of artificial lures is very common and a great entry-level to intermediate-level way to catch stripers. Jigging on the other hand (which is also an artificial) is definitely a more advanced (and effective) way to catch bass but it is much more complicated and not really a good way for someone new to the Canal to catch fish. I will discuss bait-fishing and all that goes into it.

Sides, Post Numbers, and Names

There are two more things you will quickly learn about the Canal. One is the sides, the "Cape side" verses the "Mainland side." You will often be asked, "What side were you on when you caught those fish?" (To which you quickly answer, "Don't worry about it!") You will also learn about post numbers. There are light poles that run each side of the Canal—every five poles or so there is a number posted. These numbers are used as references for specific locations. "I was at pole 180 on the Cape side." Would be a typical answer to, "Where did you catch that 60-pound stripah?"

The other thing that you will learn over time is the multitude of names there are for different areas of the Ditch. The Power Plant,

Pip's Rip, The Dolphin's, The Cribbin, The Herring Run, Mass Maritime, Bell Road, The Stone Church, Murderer's Row, you get the idea. Heck you may even end up making up a few of your own names. Let's move along.

CHAPTER 2

EQUIPMENT FOR FISHING THE CAPE COD CANAL

One of the most important things that you will learn about fishing the Cape Cod Canal is that the equipment that you use is very important. Your equipment will be your only link to a good fish when one comes your way. I know your first instinct may be to run to Wal-Mart or K-Mart to buy your fishing gear but I would strongly recommend that you hold off on that move and head more specifically to a local tackle shop and, to take it a step further, one of the great shops up around the Canal. Here is where you will find the correct equipment for your needs and they will help you on a personal level. If you're away from the Canal, read on about the equipment you may want to purchase for the Canal. The less expensive rods and reels that the big-box stores have are made with inexpensive components and will wear out very quickly, especially with the Canal's fast water and big fish. Don't go looking for the cheapest set up—you get what you pay for. That said, I wouldn't advise you to run out and buy the top-of-the-line equipment to start. Buy something decent and then continue to work your way up from there. Your needs will dictate what you should get as your interest develops.

The equipment you use is a vital link between you and the trophy bass you seek. Be sure that your "connection" is solid. Buy good quality equipment and you will not be disappointed with unexpected failure.

RODS

When fishing the Cape Cod Canal you will want to arm yourself first with a very good rod-and-reel combination. Let's cover the rod first. The rod should be between 10–11 feet long. I prefer a rod between 10-foot-six and 11 feet myself. Long rods give you very good distance and they give you power and leverage, and you will need both. There are some very good rods on the market right now that won't cost you the big bucks! You should be able to get a good entry-level rod between $125–$200. The rod is important because in the Canal your casting distance can be really important. There will be times when you won't be able to hit those fish at a distance with a rod under 10 feet.

Other criteria you will eventually look for in a rod is its power. The power of the rod can be seen in its rating. Your standard rod for throwing artificials is usually rated from either 1–3 or 4, or 2–6 ounces. For a newbie to the Ditch the 2–6 may be the way to go.

In the Canal you will in all likelihood come across some real heavyweight stripers from time to time. When this happens you are going to need a powerful rod to help you get the fish in quickly and to keep control, and the rod in your hands will have a lot to do with that. It also helps when the banks are lined with fishermen and the guys beside you are waiting to cast until you get your fish in. This is part of being a good neighbor and it is very important!

REELS

I look for three things in a reel to fish the Ditch. First, it has to have a long-cast spool. A long-cast spool holds a lot of line. The line almost falls off the reel during a cast, giving very little resistance and that means great distance. When you have big bass chasing mackerel or herring on the surface at a distance of 100 yards or more, if you don't get your lure close to that fish, you aren't catching it! Second, the reel has to have a super-smooth drag system, one capable of tiring a big fish that is hell-bent on going somewhere far from you! The final criteria is a fast crank or retrieve speed. Most reels retrieve at around 40 inches per crank, the faster the inches-per-crank you can do, the better off you will be. Any reel that cranks in 40 inches per crank or better, is what you want. You will find when fishing in the Canal that you will often have someone fishing beside you, especially when the fishing is good. When you have guys down-current and you are retrieving a lure, you often need to get your lure in fast, or "burn it in," so you don't make those guys wait too long. Being a good neighbor is important, and this is where the fast retrieve comes in very handy. Also, there will be times when you see a fish break and you will cast and miss it or you will see another fish break and you will want to cast to that one instead. You may only get one shot, remember these fish move down the current very quickly. You will need to reload almost instantly and it will require that you burn it in to get another cast off. The speed matters.

The long cast spool gives the caster a huge advantage. Notice the length of the spool. This allows for line to practically fall off the reel with little resistance during the cast. It also holds a large amount of line, making it a necessity for anyone serious about fishing the Canal.

Again you get what you pay for in a reel. A cheap reel will wear out very quickly—I have even had some fall apart in my hands. For starters you can buy an adequate "Canal" reel for somewhere between $90 and $200. When it comes to size of the reel, with a spinning reel, which I strongly suggest for an entry-level caster, you will want something between a 6000–8000 sized reel. Be sure that the reel is braid-compatible. I urge you, if you are serious about fishing the Canal, go talk to one of the local Canal shops for advice! They know the very specific details and they deal with Canal-based situations daily.

Setting the Drag

When you have hard, fast-pulling currents and sizeable fish at hand you will fight the fish with your rod and your reel in unison. The rod gives you leverage and acts as a shock absorber against the jerking and shaking of the fish's head, but your reel, and more specifically its drag system, is what will make you or break you.

The absolute worst thing you can do is leave your drag too loose. Don't let this happen! This is how you can check your drag: grab the line near the spool, wrap it around your fingers or hand a few times and pull. If the line comes off fairly easily, this is no good. You want to tighten your drag to the point that when you grab your line and pull it is fairly hard to pull it off the spool. (Be careful when doing this with braid as you will cut your hand. Wear a glove.) Now you may think this is too tight, but trust me it is not, bigger bass will dump that spool like you have no drag at all. You will need that tight drag to tire your big fish, be sure to set it correctly.

While many will tell you not to touch the drag during a fight, if the line is dumping too quickly, you will have to tighten your drag knob. Do so by turning it clockwise a quarter-turn at a time until you have it tight enough to battle the fish correctly. If absolutely necessary you could also apply external drag by cupping the spool gently with your hand, increasing resistance. Conversely if you have the drag too tight, and the fish is pulling you to where you are being pulled off balance, you may have to loosen the drag. Remember that an over-tightening the drag could easily lead to rod or line breakage. It is a fine line, so don't overlook this important detail.

LINE

The line you use matters. Let's first talk briefly about monofilament. Monofilament line is a thing of the past. If you are not using one of the "super braids" then you need to experience a life change. In short, braided lines are limp, soft and pliable which means they cast great. The line just falls off the spool, as opposed to banging off the top of the spool causing resistance and loss of distance. Second is diameter. The diameter of braided line is so small it gives you much greater casting distance. For example, 30-pound braid is the equivalent to the size of 8-pound test monofilament. That's pretty small. When casting distance matters, 30-pound test is as small as I will go, because anything smaller is impossible to handle—it is like thread at that point.

One of the things I really love about braid is that it has zero stretch, so hooksets are instantaneous. If you moved the rod tip six inches, the lure moves six inches. Fishing mono used to be like fishing with a long rubber band, the stretch definitely impacted the hook-set. The no-stretch line also means that sensitivity is extremely good.

With braid, I can feel everything and that's the way I like it. One more positive that braid offers is that it has no memory. Remember when the mono would come off the spool and it would look like a Slinky blew up? And then to make things worse it would twist up making a huge mess! Those days are gone. Braid is the answer.

Now with all that said, when you make the move to braid, you have to give yourself time to get used to it. In terms of sensitivity, fishing mono is like wearing gloves to pick up tooth picks; fishing braid is like using your bare fingers to pick up pencils. It is that different!

For fishing the Canal here are some suggestions for what size braid to use. The standard braid is 40–50 pound test. For added casting distance you may want to drop down to 30 pound test. Fishermen jigging with heavier equipment may often use 50–70 pound test because of the rocks and the tangles. Also in the Canal you will want to spool up with no less than 300 yards of line.

Lastly, braid can cut you. When using braid you will want to use some sort of finger protection, either waterproof tape, a glove, a single-finger glove or something similar.

THE CONNECTION: LEADERS AND CLIPS

At the business end of your braid, you are going to need a leader and a clip of some sort to attach your lure to. The leader is your final connection between your braid and your lure. I attach the leader to the running line (braid) using a barrel swivel. The barrel swivel I recommend is a Spro Size 2, rated at 230 pounds. Krok is also a well-respected brand. I connect the barrel to the braid using a Palomar knot. I use a monofilament leader, called "leader material," usually somewhere between 60 and 80 pound test. Why so heavy? Why not? Why take a chance on losing a big fish because your leader breaks or because a 30-pound leader ran across some rip-rap and broke off your fish. Most importantly I use the heavy leader for handling. Braid will cut you very quickly and deep. Any mono over 40 pound test will not. When securing a fish, you want to wrap the leader around your hand and pull it up out of the water and onto the rocks. At that point, you are safe—and extremely overjoyed.

On the end of the leader you want something to attach the lure to. On the market now are fast clips, which look like a paper clip—in the old days we used Duo Locks. The fast clips offer the ability to change lures very quickly. Backlash Sportfishing and Tactical Angler make the two dominant clips on the market. For the Canal I'd go with Backlash's 150 pound test XL clip or TA's 125-pound clip. When it comes time to attach your leader to your clip or your leader to your barrel swivel you will want to use a simple cinch knot, especially with the heavy leader material. Through the eye, wrap three times around the running line and then back through the hole, done. There is no need to improve this knot, which would be overkill.

Leader length should be between 30 and 36 inches on an 11-foot rod. It cannot be longer than that or you will have problems with your back-cast. It can't be too short, either, because you need a leader long enough for you to handle and get control of a fish at your feet, with enough length to grab onto.

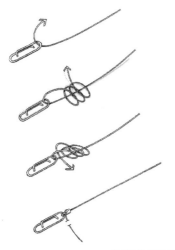

This is the simple cinch knot. It can be used with any monofilament leader material, 40 pound test or over. No need to improve this knot. Go through the eye, back out and around three times, and then back through the loop. Cinch it down and you have the strongest knot that you can ask for.

ARTIFICIAL LURES

As you learn the various aspects of fishing the Canal, it will seem like you need a multitude of lures, plugs, or artificial offerings for the constantly changing situations that unfold in front of you. In brief, you do not have to buy every lure that you hear about or are told that you have to buy. We will cover lure selection and usage in detail in Chapter 3. We will discuss what lures to put into the bag and more importantly what to pull out and when, and will try to lift the haze of confusion that comes when deciding what lure to use.

Your arsenal is very important as you will see as you develop. Lure selection can be very important!

FOOTWEAR

Footwear is terribly important at the Ditch because just about everywhere you will stand is on rocks, commonly called rip-rap. Wet rocks are very slippery and very dangerous. Sliding and falling is almost a given without the correct footwear. I have seen falls that resulted in broken bones and compound fractures—why do that to yourself? Many of the guys that fish the Ditch just wear a simple rubber knee boot such as those made by Servus or Marlin. The regulars often times buy them a size bigger than what fits so that if the unfortunate happens and you fall into the drink, you can kick them off quickly, giving you a chance at recovery. My strong recommendation, especially if you are new or unsure of yourself, is to throw a pair of Korkers on. Korkers are a hard rubber sandal that has a studded cleat, small metal spikes that when worn, give you a solid, non-slip grip when down in the slime zone. They get strapped on to the bottom of your boots and they make a huge difference.

Personally I mostly wear stocking-foot chest waders when fishing the Canal, the same ones I wear all season long in my travels when I am not wetsuiting. I use these for a couple of reasons. They keep me dry and clean and at lower ends of the tide I can get out in some places and stand in shin deep water, not having to worry about hanging up on my back-cast. With the stocking foot waders I wear felt-soled wading boots. The felt soles alone are very good on slimy, wet rocks. Into the felt soles I screw small metal spikes. The studs I use are called Grip Studs, and you install them with a special tool (you can find them all online). The specific stud I like is the #1100. I cannot emphasize how much I like and trust these studs! I wear them all season long, from April until Christmas. The studs I have on my boots presently, I have worn going on three years now, they don't wear out easily and that's huge.

For those that wear a boot foot wader, or stocking foot for that matter, it may not be a bad idea to keep a knife on your belt just in case the worst happens and you fall into the drink, you can cut yourself free. My best advice however is wear the right foot-wear, be extremely careful, and don't fall in in the first place. In warmer weather, sometimes shorts with just the wader boots also works nicely.

THE CANAL BIKE

The next piece of equipment that you may want to consider is a Canal Bike, a bike rigged up for fishing the Canal. Such a bike is a luxury and not a necessity. The step-through frame (like a girl's bike) is widely popular for getting on and off the bike quickly and without hanging up two important friends. There are many variations on the Canal Bike but the basic one would have a couple of tubes for carrying rods, baskets on each side for carrying things like a plugbag, a fish, foul weather gear or your lunch, oh and please . . . definitely stow your garbage. It would also not be a bad idea to stash an extra tire tube and pump, just in case you get a flat seven miles from where you parked.

The bike allows you to cover a lot of ground. A lot of fellows use the bike to cruise the path and spot breaking fish, at which point they run down and make a couple of casts. Others use the bike simply to get away from crowded areas and find a quieter place to fish, this would be my primary reason for the bike.

You want to be sure that when you put your rod tubes on your bike that you do your best to keep them straight up and down. You don't want them to point out in the back because they will hit other rods or things when you turn. You also don't want to do a rooster tail, or fan the rods across the back. This will cause you to hit other rods on bikes coming the other way or when you pass. (www.johndoblephotography.com)

The bike serves the same purpose as a beach buggy, a great tool for fishing and for covering ground. However the bike, much like the buggy, can make a man lazy. Instead of being in the water, in work mode, making casts and working up a fish or two, you can become lazy and just watch for a bent rod and then decide to fish that spot. Don't fish like this. It isn't right to be mugging guys that have been fishing a spot, putting in their time, only to get crowded out when they hook up by a guy who runs down the bank or even worse, casts from the service road.

A smart biker would see the guys below hooked up and then move down a couple of hundred yards in the direction that the fish are moving, find a spot, and then get down to water level and be ready to cast when they come by.

WADERBELT

In all surfcasting situations I strongly recommend a waderbelt. With any waderbelt I strongly suggest a pair of pliers with a lanyard and sheath. The best wader belt is made of the same material as a dive belt, a real tough nylon webbing. The waderbelt is a necessity for safety, when cinched tight around your waist over your waders, it will keep water from pouring into your wader should you fall into the water, giving you time to recover. Other than that it is like what a tool belt is to a carpenter. You wear it everywhere, all the time. If you are fishing with just shorts on and a T-shirt or if you are fishing fully geared up, you will always have your most important tool, your pliers, right where you can get them quickly. You can put numerous things onto your belt along with your pliers. A water bottle, some plugbags or pouches, and you can carry a Boga grip on a D-ring, which I do as I like to release my bass. It is nice to get a weight before releasing the big girl, "Wow 58 pounds?? That's great!!"

Wearing a plugbag and waderbelt gives you everything you need within reach. Putting your pliers on a lanyard keeps you from losing them should they drop.

PLUGBAG

I think every person that fishes the surf, even marginally, needs a plugbag. You should have a bag to carry your lures in as you head out to the water's edge. You never know exactly what a new session on the water will require. A plugbag is another piece of equipment that can range from a small bag that will carry three or four plugs and cost thirty bucks, to a ridiculously over-sized suitcase-like bag that holds fifty lures. I prefer to do things practically and as easily as possible. When fishing the Ditch most guys will carry a shoulder bag, which works fine. I wear two plug bags on my waderbelt in which I carry enough plugs that I expect will suit my needs for that particular session. Again we will cover what goes into your plugbag in Chapter 3. A couple other plugbag considerations would be a file to sharpen hooks, a plastic tape measure, and maybe a basic fish-gripper.

BUG SPRAY

Bug spray is an absolute necessity when fishing the Ditch. Not having any can easily put you into the Psycho Unit at the nearest hospital on short order. The only thing more distracting than a mosquito assault when you are trying to catch the big one is having a guy near you that thinks out loud. I usually slather up while I am gearing up, I also keep a small bottle of bug spray in my plugbag, for when a pesky situation arises.

CHAPTER 3

LURE SELECTION

The lure that you decide to attach to the end of your line can, in fishing terms, give you one of the best experiences that you can have, with feelings unrivaled by almost anything in this world. The fight, the drag singing to you, the bend of the rod, the water spray in the face, white knuckles, and finally you see the body of a huge fish—the taking of a great fish can be euphoric. Now on the other hand, a bad decision can break a man's spirit, bring nightmares and sleeplessness for months. The lure you choose can make you or break you.

While there is no magic lure that fits all needs, there are lures that give you high percentage shots at success. I want to try to give you some of those options in this chapter.

The most important trait a lure has is its ability to give you confidence. In fishing, having confidence in what you are throwing, and knowing that if a fish sees it, it will strike it, is huge. If I could give you a lure and I told you that this lure will catch fish, that this is the lure you must have, you would probably pay me $50 for it, right? It is better to have one or two lures that you feel really good

The lure you decide to throw, and the way you present it, can make the difference between a day when you go home with nothing or a nice mid-30 pound class like the one shown here.

about and know intimately, than having 23 that you have no idea about and bought just because you read somewhere that they are what you need.

There is no worse feeling in the world than standing in between two guys that are catching fish after fish and you can't hook up. To make things even worse, you don't have the same lure that they have, you are not even in the ballpark. Thus the importance of lure selection weighs heavy. One thing I would like to emphasize is that when you do get a new lure, take it down and throw it and thoroughly learn its action and the best way to work it, that way when it is game on and there are fish all over the place, you are not left scrabbling wondering the best way to work this lure. Watching your lure and learning its swim, will give you much needed confidence.

LONG RANGE

Your long range lures will in all likelihood be poppers. You will cast these to breaking fish that you see on the surface, commonly called sight-casting. Long distance casting to water where there may be fish but you don't see them, is called blind casting. These casts are what I call "bombs," that is your longest possible cast. The lures you will be casting in these situations will normally be between 3 and 4 ounces, these are optimal casting weights with the long rod that you will be using. Remember, distance matters!

Of the poppers there are two primary ones, the Polaris popper and the pencil popper. The Polaris popper can also be called a "bottle popper." It is cast out and then chugged back in at intervals. The timing of those intervals will be determined by you. The object is to throw water and get the fish's attention. The commotion will draw the fish.

The next popper is the pencil popper. This is a great long casting lure that when worked correctly, imitates a wounded, fleeing bait fish, an easy target for a feeding striper.

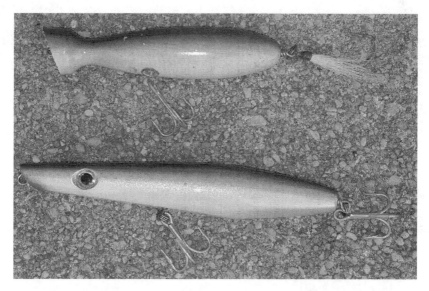

Here are two commonly used poppers, the Polaris popper (top) and the pencil popper. The two poppers are used with two different retrieve techniques.

One other long range lure would be a tin, or metal. For the distance you would need something heavier, anything between 2 and 5 ounces. You can cast this out and retrieve it, or you can cast it out, let it sink for a decent amount of time, and then retrieve it. This can be a very effective way to catch nice fish in the Canal.

SHORT RANGE

You will also have opportunities to catch bass point blank, at your feet or very nearby. At this point you will be able to use a variety of lures that are more fish-like or that "match the hatch" a little better. Long range casting is more about commotion and drawing attention, while short range is more about finesse. With that said, when bass are blitzing bait and they have it pinned up against the side of the Canal, you can throw just about anything and it will be whacked, a hot dog with a hook in it will work. But other times, when the bass are more on the prowl, you will need to fool them with something that looks more "fishy." Now the lure you choose may well be the difference between scoring or going home with no fish. We will cover all of your lure options here in Chapter Three. We will discuss your tactics and approach in Chapter Four.

I recall a day at the Canal when I ran across a couple of guys just coming up the trail. We exchanged hello's and I asked the common question: how did you do? The answer was over the top, great! The one fellow emphasized to me that the bass were on mackerel and if the lure didn't have vertical lines on it, the bass weren't interested. Is it surprising that a bass would react in such a way? Yes and no. You would figure that a hungry, feeding fish would eat anything that looked even remotely like a fish, and I believe that to be largely true. However there are times when stripers become very focused on one specific detail, as in this case with the mackerel stripes. Keep in mind that sometimes there are specific characteristics that bass look for and you may need a specific color or shaped artificial in order to produce a hit.

TOP CANAL ARTIFICIALS

I am going to provide a list of lures that I believe you should have and I will try to explain why you will need them. Remember that different lures are used for different situations, and how these situations unfold before you has an impact. Sometimes the fish will be way out at the end of your cast and will require a certain lure, and sometimes they may be at your feet and that will require quite a different lure. A bright day, or an overcast day, or even darkness may come into play. What bait they are on will also come into play and there are many different plugs that mimic the various baitfish.

The Gibbs Polaris Popper/Super Strike Little Neck Popper

You'll see this lure quite a bit while fishing on the Canal, and it has taken a large number of fish. Cast it straight out as far as you can, then chug it in against the current. Chug—reel tight, chug—reel tight, chug—reel tight. You will figure out your correct cadence and speed of retrieve. The goal is to throw water and spray all over the area, drawing stripers to what they think is a wounded baitfish waddling across the surface, an easy target. Most guys fish the Polaris by casting it straight out long and then chugging it back in with hard strokes and in a rhythm as it sweeps in the current.

The Magic Swimmer

I don't remember another lure that gained so much popularity so fast after its introduction. It is not unusual to see this lure hanging off numerous rods when down at the Ditch. If you fish the Canal you have to have at least two of these in your stash. It is divided into three segments, which causes it to swim with such fluidity, looks so natural, and is so well balanced that it really looks like a herring swimming along without a worry in the world. This is why it accounts for good numbers of fish, as stripers love to hit them. This particular lure comes in fast- sinking or slow-sinking. In the Ditch the slow-sinking is the most popular for your short game, casting within 50 yards of the bank. When it comes to retrieving, this lure is hard to screw up, you can burn it in (reel it in as fast as you can), or you can work it medium to slow, injecting twitches and allowing it to drop back a little on occasion. Both retrieves work well. Come up with a retrieve that works for you. Have some fun!

The Magic Swimmer is one of the top producers on the Canal. By watching it swim you will soon know why it is so popular!

Now an important tip on the Magic Swimmer. You have to change the hooks as soon as you get it, because the hooks aren't made for saltwater. I remove both hooks using split ring pliers and I put on a 3/0 VMC treble to the belly. I don't use a tailhook with this lure but you can also use a flag (just some bucktail with no hook). For split rings go with a 5.5H.

The Pencil Popper

The pencil popper is my personal favorite lure for fishing the Cape Cod Canal. The number of big fish I have taken on pencils is simply amazing. While it may be one of the more complicated lures to learn and work, I can say with certainty that it is the most effective. The pencil popper comes in a wide range of sizes, more specifically lengths or weights. At times the smaller pencil is all the bass will want, perhaps 5-inches and 1½ ounces, at other times the bigger pencils are needed, 9–10 inches weighing closer to 4 ounces. The size will depend on the size of the bait present and how far you need to cast. The best all-around weight is probably between 2–2¾ ounces. You pull out the heavyweights, poppers 3½ ounces and up, when the bait is large or when you need extra distance.

There are two styles of pencil popper, the standard pencil which is completely round, the other being what has been labeled, "the Canal Style," which is a flat bottomed pencil made to reduce resistance and made to slide across the top of fast current at places such as—you guessed it—the Canal, thus the name.

Before we move on, an important point on fishing poppers, specifically on setting the hook. Getting this right could mean the

LURE SELECTION   53

difference between a fishless morning and a respectable morning
with several fish caught and released. When you are retrieving a
popper and you see a bass waking behind it, taking shots at the lure,
it is easy to lose your composure in the excitement. Don't panic,
be patient! If what you were doing got a bass trailing your popper,
don't change anything. Keep doing your thing, let the bass do its
thing. Wait until you feel the heaviness of the fish—that is when
you want to set the hook. Remember it is based on what you feel,
not anything you see. When you react visually you run a very good
chance of pulling the lure away from the bass or spooking the fish,
because you changed something that worked previously. Be patient
and be smart.

WORKING THE PENCIL

Regardless of the pencil's size or style, you work it the same
way. Fairly quick action as opposed to slow, and you want it
slapping across the surface in a side-to-side motion with its
back end anchored and acting as a fulcrum. Slap-slap-slap-
slap, left-right, left-right, left-right, and I do mean slapping.
It is the slapping that draws the attention of the fish. Working
a pencil is all about rhythm and cadence. The mistake I see
guys make with it is reeling too slow and "snaking" it across
the surface the way a snake slithers through the grass.

After you cast, you want to stand straight up with your rod
butt between your thighs and your rod tip almost straight up.
If you are right handed, you will stand with your left hand on
the handle of the reel and your right hand just above the reel

seat. As you are retrieving you will gently shake or wiggle the rod with the right, while reeling with your left hand just fast enough to keep the lure slapping. There is a lot of hand–eye coordination needed here and practice will make perfect. Master this technique and good things will follow.

To work a pencil popper properly, for the right-handed caster, the rod butt goes between the legs and the right hand is placed above the reel and gently shakes the rod while the left-hand slow-reels. The pencil should slap the water violently, while moving left and right.

Daiwa SP Minnow

This is a hard plastic swimmer, 6-inches long, that swims just below the surface in a fast little wiggle. This lure has taken the surfcasting community at large the same way the Magic Swimmer has taken over the Canal. This is a great, universally acclaimed lure that can be fished anywhere at any time. It is one of the few lures that can probably be fished exclusively for an entire season. But who would do that? You would put the tackle shops out of business.

It casts ridiculously well for its size, and that is probably because it has a weight transfer system, that allows you to cast it 40–50 yards when necessary, with relative ease. This lure can seriously catch fish. The one issue with the SP Minnow is that its factory hooks and split rings are not capable of holding a fish over 18 pounds. Thus when you buy one you have to immediately change the splits and hooks before putting it into service. You can use it and you will catch fish out of the package, but if you do have the fortune of hitting a nice fish, your chances of landing it are low—you are more likely to have some straightened hooks and tears rolling down your cheeks. The nice thing about the SP is that you can change the hooks and use various size hooks and it still swims like a champ! One spring we were catching a lot of big bass in the surf off the beaches and the SP is all they wanted, so we upsized the hooks to 4/0 trebles, and it still worked great.

What colors . . . .? In the Canal, the blue and green mackerel are a lock. It would not be a bad idea to have a yellow or chicken scratch in case there are bunker, peanut or adult. Bone is always a consistent choice and I love blurple in the dark.

REMEMBER—WATCH YOUR WEIGHT

We will be touching on some of the higher weight lures. Once you get over four ounces you have to be sure that the rating on your rod is capable of throwing the heavier weights. Failure to do so can result in rod breakage.

The Paddletail Shad

The rubber paddletail shad is a super-efficient bass catcher in any venue, including the Big Ditch, so it's wise to have a couple in your bag. The leading brand in swim shads is Tsunami. They make great shads and for me they rule the shad roost! The great thing about fishing a shad is that it is fail-proof, you can't mess it up on the retrieve. Do not make the common mistake that newcomers make by reeling too fast (that's true with any lure for that matter), a moderate retrieve will do nicely, an occasional twitch works good too. Another thing I really like about the shad is it casts easily and it can penetrate the water column fairly well when allowed to sink. My hands-down favorite in paddletail shads are Tsunami Swim Shads, most every tackle shop has them. Tsunami has multiple Swim Shads sizes ranging from 2-inch up to 10-inch. I would start with the 6-inch (2⅜ ounce) shad and then go up or down as needed. My second choice may be up to the 7-inch (3-ounce) which has a considerably stronger hook for when there are cows in front of you. When there are big fish in front of you I would suggest not throwing the 6-inch and under as the hook may not hold a giant in the fast currents.

The other popular swim shad by Tsunami is the Deep Shad which both casts great and gets deep very quickly. It comes in 5-inch, 3 ounce, or the 6½-inch, 4¼-ounce size, both awesome in certain situations.

Now on to the next question, what color? I have two basic colors that I carry, the Golden Bunker and the Pearl with the spot. These two have always served me well, that said I don't usually get crazy about color except when the fish do. When in doubt, natural colors will always serve you well, black-back, blue-back or olive-back. Remember that when the fish go on the feed, and they are hitting anything with reckless abandon, color goes and sits in the backseat.

Savage Sandeel

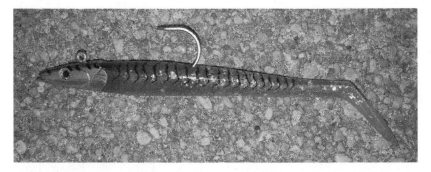

The Savage Sandeel is widely effective at the Ditch as it mimics numerous baits that run through the Canal.

I have to mention the Savage Sandeel, which right now is the biggest thing to hit the Canal since the Magic Swimmer. This rubber paddletail comes as a leadhead with an interchangeable body. It comes in many sizes and weights, the most common weights being between 2–5 ounces. The weight you use will depend on how deep you want to go, how fast the current is pulling, how hard the wind is blowing. Three to four and a half ounces is a good choice for starters. Color-wise green and blue mackerel are very popular followed closely by pearl. Remember also that when you go up in weight, especially into the 4 and 5 ounces, be sure your rod is capable of throwing those weights.

Leadhead/Rubber Combo and Bucktails

When it comes to choosing leadheads and bucktails for fishing the Canal, you could ask ten fishermen what brand or style they like best and get ten different answers.

What this tells you is that this is a universal lure, and frankly presentation is more important than what brand to buy. You need a lure that you can make do what you need it to do and in this case it's about fishing deep. When we talk depth we talk weight—your choice on what you buy will come down to how much weight you need. This will be discussed in more detail in Chapters 4 and 5.

In my fishing, outside of the Canal, leadhead/rubber lures and bucktails are my go-to lures almost anywhere I fish. I can tell you the exact brand I fish of everything I use, but these specifics are not really important. So I will speak in general terms as far as that is concerned but I will echo what others have suggested too as starting points for you. Eventually you will find different lures in this category that you really favor. It may be because you catch the biggest bass you ever caught on one particular lure, or it may be that you find extra confidence in a particular color or style. If

Bucktails, known as "barracudas" by the old school, are a great weapon in your Canal arsenal. Here Mitsu Sfougaris gives you some proof with a 48-pound striper. (www.johndoblephotography.com)

in Canal country I would strongly suggest stopping into one of the great tackle shops and getting some info and intel. Some of the notable names that I have come across are: JoeBaggs, Andrus, Lunker City, B&D, Bill Hurley, Gag's, and there are many more. Color-wise the consensus says white, yellow, or black. Personally I favor chartreuse.

When it comes to weight for bucktails or leadhead combo's, we are shooting for penetration so I would start with 2 ounces and go up to 4 ounces for your initial learning period. Remember that going higher than 4-ounces would mean a different rod/reel set-up, and will be discussed in detail in Chapter 5. The color you choose is up to you, and it may depend on what bait is in front of you, but going with two basic colors is always good, white or black. Some other color options would be chartreuse, yellow, or blue. Please also note that I am not addressing "jigging" the Ditch, but rather for more all-around use and for getting down into the water column where fish may be feeding, rather than closer to the surface.

Stick Shad/Stick Baits

We also need to cover stick baits, stick shads, or glide baits, and I mention these because they have been productive for me and others.

These lures are cast out and retrieved with a moderate to fast retrieve with several hard jerks, then a slight pause to give the lure a slashing, darting movement, then fast again to another series of jerks and pause. You stay in contact with the lure throughout the retrieve. Retrieving this lure is something that you will really need to practice, watching it swim and get its optimal movement under wraps. This is a suspending, gliding lure, which means it sinks and suspends horizontally, which allows you to make it dart and slash easily. This lure looks awesome in the water when fished correctly.

Surf Asylum makes some very good stick and glide baits that work very well in the Canal. Also the Sebile-style Stick Shad is super.

Darters

You can't talk about hard pulling currents without mentioning darters or, as they call them at the Ditch, "datas." Darters thrive in fast water—they have a tight little wiggle with some notable and deliberate side-to-side darts back and forth. The make or brand will dictate the darting action as well as how deep they swim. When you cast out, begin reeling, then sweep the rod tip to get the darter to grab and dig—you will feel it when it happens. There are many brands out there Super Strike, Gibbs, Asylum, Wally's, Tactical Angler, and Linesider69 to name a few good ones. This is another lure that you will need to watch as it swims to learn the action and how it handles the current of the Ditch.

CANAL PLUGBAG SELECTION

Here is a list of suggested lures for your Canal plugbag. (*mandatory)

1. *Magic Swimmer, fast or slow sink.
2. *Guppy Pencil, 3 ounce, green mackerel.
3. *Daiwa SP Minnow, blue mackerel.
4. *Savage Sandeel, 2–5 ounces.
5. *3-ounce Tsunami Fat Shad-Pearl.
6. *Canal Stick Shad, white.
7. 4-ounce leadhead w/9-inch Slug-Go, black.
8. 3-ounce white bucktail with Otter Tail.
9. Wally's Pencil, 3-ounce, yellow mackerel.
10. 3½ ounce Gibb's Polaris popper, yellow.

CHAPTER 4

STRATEGIES FOR FISHING THE CAPE COD CANAL

When you have a fishery as big, diverse, and complex as the Cape Cod Canal, coming up with a simple recipe for success here is not easy. Its deep waters and fast-moving currents add quite a dimension to the game. There are very few similar situations in standard surfcasting.

THE LONG GAME VERSUS THE SHORT GAME

I am going to break fishing the Canal down into two categories or strategies. The long game, which would include casting out to fish towards the middle of the Canal, and the short game where you have bass anywhere from at your feet or in very close to you, out to 30 yards. There are also times when stripers push huge schools of bait through the Canal in a universal and unified attack, where they will feed continuously in unison everywhere and anywhere, out deep and in tight.

Bait wants to ball up for safety—the old adage of "safety in numbers" comes to mind. The striper wants to wreak havoc and chaos in the hard pulling currents of the Ditch, breaking up the bait school and using the hard currents to keep the bait scattered and unable to regroup. As the bait breaks off the schools, they get singled out by bass one-on-one. This is where your fun begins.

THE SURFACE

Poppers

A lot of your fishing when the aforementioned happens takes place on the surface, where you can actually see bass swirling and chasing a bait fish across the surface. A keen eye can give you a huge advantage. It is very important to be vigilant and watch what is happening upstream. Look for breaking fish—sometimes the gulls will tip you off as well as they swirl and hover over top of the activity. Watch everything! There will be times when the activity will be out beyond casting distance, but other times it will be well within your range. Your object when this happens is to use an artificial to distract the bass, pull its attention off the panicked mackerel or herring and onto your pencil or Polaris popper. This is known as sight casting. With this technique you watch and wait when fish are moving through, then make your cast at a precise moment. Your cast has to be on target—you have to land your lure about 20 feet in front of the last seen breach. Remember that these fish are moving quickly and a lot of times you will only get off one cast, so make it a good one! If you miss you have to reel all the way back in and then recast and that takes valuable time. This is where the high-speed retrieve that we talked about comes in handy. This is where everything that you have read about in this book to this point comes together. Long, accurate casts are now vitally important. Long rods, good line, smooth drags, and good-casting lures will help you land a good bass.

Big bass love properly presented pencils, especially when the fish are focused and are on the feed. The great thing about the Canal is you never know—your next cast maybe your biggest bass ever!

One day while fishing with one of my buddies, we were waiting for another slug of fish to push through, taking a little break. There were patches of foam floating by from time to time, and he would make a cast and try to hit the foam with his lure. He was working on his accuracy, not a bad idea! He was a good caster and made it look a lot easier than it is. Try it some time—practice makes perfect.

Let me mention one more thing here and that is size and color of your lures, specifically pencil poppers and Polaris poppers. The Polaris has a very distinguishable, universal body shape (see photo on page 48) and the two most popular brands are Gibbs and Super Strike. Super Strike calls their style the Little Neck and is made of plastic. The age-old Gibbs are most popular. They are made of wood and the 3½ ounce is favored. The former will sink, the latter floats. One other aspect to these poppers is the size of the face and the depth of the concave—both Gibbs and Super Strike are moderate and adequate. Some people prefer a bigger face or a deeper concave, because the deeper the concave, the more water you will throw, and when you throw more water you draw more attention. That could be a good thing, but the deep concave can also slow you down quite a bit and add a lot more resistance to your retrieve, which I am not crazy about because it becomes more like work and less like fishing. It's also possible that throwing too much water will spook the fish. I favor a more moderate concavity, but when fishing is really slow I will often begin my retrieve with real hard strokes, causing a lot of water displacement, commotion, and sound in order to draw fish.

As mentioned, I am a pencil-popper freak, it is probably my favorite lure and I use one whenever I can, all season long. Some of the best out there today are Guppy's, Afterhours, Wally's, Striper Maine-iac, and Gibbs to name a few big names. The sizes can range from 1-ounce up to 4-ounces and from 4-inches up to 8-inches or better. Most of the time the 2–3 ounce range will be suitable. Sometimes the bass get fussy and you will be forced to go down to a smaller pencil (2-ounces and less), so be sure you have one handy. I have been caught without the smaller poppers several times and it hurts when others are banging and you can't get a hook-up.

Mackerel Imitators—The Super Strike Zig-Zag darter (top) and the Striper Maine-iac pencil popper both have the look you want when the mackerel are running roughshod over the Canal. Sometimes those stripes make all the difference.

Color choice would depend on the bait present and what the bass are feeding on. When herring are moving through I prefer blue-back, pink sides and white belly. For bunker or pogie the color is yellow or gold. For mackerel that are swimming for their lives, any color will work as long as the lure has the vertical, black mackerel stripes on the sides, the most common being blue and green. My personal favorites are yellow mackerel and pink mackerel.

The Short Game—Surface Swimmers

When things go crazy in the Canal you will have some great things to watch, as bass chase bait right up onto the rocks around you. The bass will be too close for poppers as you can't cast that short, so it is a good time for surface swimmers. One of my favorites would be a metal-lip swimmer. The metal-lip swimmer is not a great casting lure but in this case it doesn't have to be. It will swim slowly and deliberately across the surface, leaving a nice big wake and telling the fish below to "EAT ME!" It doesn't get much better than watching a striper smack a metal lip. There are several good ones on the market—find one that works in the Canal and stuff it into your bag. When shopping just be sure that it will hold in fast moving water.

One of the best all-surface, hard-plastic swimmers that is readily available is the Cotton-Cordell 7-inch Red Fin. This plug shines in the Canal.

Other near surface swimmers are also handy, most of these are hard plastic swimmers. My personal favorite would be the loaded Cotton Cordell Red Fin, which casts great and swims just below the surface and has been a personal staple of mine for decades. Other choices would be the Daiwa SP Minnow, or a slow-sinking Magic Swimmer, or any of the hard plastic swimmers, and there are many varieties on the market. One important warning about most of these lures, when you buy them, their cheap factory hooks and split rings will not hold good fish, and thus they must be changed. Most lures use 5.5H split rings and 3/0 VMC treble hooks; for the Canal you may want to bump up to a 4/0 to give you a little more strength. The SP Minnow requires a smaller 4H split ring.

Holy Mackerel!! Seeing bait at your feet is not uncommon in the Canal. Looking down and seeing something like a couple mackerel hugging the rocks is usually a sign that the bass are on the prowl. Be sure you wear polarized sunglasses to enable you to see clearly into the water without the glare of the sun. It makes a huge difference!

BELOW THE SURFACE

So if you can see bass chasing a bait across the surface, imagine what is going on beneath the surface! In all likelihood you have bass chasing individual baits all over the water column, near the surface, mid-column and near the bottom. A keyword here will be penetration. Drop down an acceptable offering, present it properly and good things will happen. One of the keys to this is letting your lure sink. I know this sounds simplistic but many, many guys I see don't wait for their lure to sink. In fast moving current, and in deep water, let's say 25 feet or more, you want to get it deep and it will take some patience to get your lure down. It is at this time where you may want to throw some sort of a leadhead. They cast well and they sink well and they present a nice profile to bass.

Penetration

One morning after some good action I walked back to my vehicle and in the lot I found a couple of guys, who looked like a father son duo. They had two nice big bass laying on the ground, both fish pushing 30 pounds. I gave them a quick greeting and a thumbs-up and I started walking away. At about my fourth step I stopped and asked, "what did you get them on?" The older gentleman held up a Cotton-Cordell pencil popper. He handed me the pencil popper, and when I took it I almost dropped it as its weight caught me off guard. "Wow! That's heavy!" He went on to tell me that they load them with shot, and they don't fish them like conventional pencils but rather cast them out, count to ten, and then reel back in "sloooowly," letting the lure sway in the current. The fish mistake it as a wounded or dying fish and they inhale it. It was a great tip! I made several of these lures and have used them successfully, not only in the Canal but in many other situations, especially where I needed long casts and deep penetration.

Bucktails and Leadheads and Jigging

When the hit in the Canal is hot, poppers usually rule the roost because there is no better sight in the world than watching bass smack a popper on the surface. But when things begin to return to normal a good penetrating lure becomes relevant, so let's talk about bucktails and leadhead/rubber combinations.

Jigging the Canal is a huge part of the Canal fishery. So huge in fact I did a separate chapter on it. It is an advanced tactic and requires special equipment which is out of the scope of this chapter, but it does need to be addressed.

Jigging the Canal is done with a heavy set up, a rod rated up to six or eight ounces is the norm, sometimes 10–12, perhaps considered a pool cue by some. The rod has to be stiff enough to cast decent weights out a good way from shore, and strong enough to pull big bass out of the holes or away from the bridge abutments. A good-sized spinning reel is also required and many of the guys that jig the Canal on a regular basis use a conventional reel. Heavier braids are also favored, the most common being 50 to 70-pound braid. On the business end, four and five ounce bucktails or leadheads with rubber attached are common. The key to jigging is staying on, bouncing along the bottom for as long as you can and working the contour of the bottom, concentrating preferably on drop-offs and holes. Over time and hard work you learn what to look for and where to fish. You will learn that you want to be at certain holes at certain stages of the tide. This is also where the post numbers work to your advantage for marking spots. So let's pan out a little bit.

Commonly when you hit the Canal you want your arsenal to consist of some bucktails and leadhead/rubber combo's and your goal is for fish that are mid-column, from five feet below the surface to a few feet off the bottom. I recommend bucktails between 1.5–4 ounces for this section of the column. When you combine a leadhead with rubber you are now looking at offerings between 2.5 and 5 ounces. By throwing these and becoming comfortable with them you are not only allowing yourself the chance to get some fish and build your confidence, but also giving yourself a gateway to jigging the bottom.

When working a bucktail or leadhead/rubber combo, you want to basically mimic a baitfish swimming happily along while it is trying to stay in control in the fast-moving currents. Once you cast out, let it sink and penetrate the water column, then reel super fast to catch up (or reel to contact), then reel slow, only enough to stay in touch with the offering. You don't have to reel it in immediately. Let it swim deep in the fast-sweeping currents of the Ditch. Give a deep-holding fish a chance to get a look at it.

CHAPTER 5

JIGGING THE CAPE COD CANAL

Jigging in the Canal is a more advanced technique—I would not advise a beginner to jump into this, because an angler needs a thorough understanding of the currents and water movements to be good at jigging, and it takes time fishing the Canal to develop this kind of knowledge. Jigging requires heavy equipment, rods, reels, and line, and heavy offerings to present to striped bass that congregate on the bottom. The bottom of the Canal is not flat. It is covered mostly with rock and rubble and in some areas it is sand. It has a rolling contour and it has holes forged by strong currents and bridge abutments, altogether making mountains and valleys over which the current roars. The bass like to sit in the depressions, or valleys, where they do not have to fight the direct current, and as the bait gets swept over them, a bass simply shoots up and grabs it, and then retreats back from whence it came. And although I am obviously talking about the Cape Cod Canal, what I am describing here is relevant to any fast, deep-water canal, inlet, or river.

Jimmy Ellinas touts a beautiful striper, 55½ pounds that he pulled from the strong currents of the Big Ditch, using a jig. (www.johndoblephotography).

The whole objective with jigging is getting the jig into the face of the fish—it has to be close in order to get a reaction. When I do seminars, I like to use the example of a basketball hoop, which sits

10 feet off the ground. Pretend you are standing under the rim and you are standing on the bottom of the river or Canal, and the surface was the hoop, ten feet above you. The bass is sitting at about shin level, waiting to be fed by what I call "the conveyor belt," or the strong current that carries bait. If a bait came across the surface, 9 feet above the bass, what do you think the chances would be of that bass going up to hit that bait? Now what if that bait came at one to two feet off the floor (bottom), right in the fish's wheelhouse? Now what are the chances of that bass hitting the offering? Now of course the Canal is a lot deeper than 10 feet, on average 25–40 feet deep. That kind of depth adds to the complexity of getting a presentation down and still controlling and "feeling" what your jig is doing. Remember now you are not going straight down, you have to factor in a very strong current. The current is what makes the conveyor belt work.

So you have the mountains and valleys and you have the conveyor belt, now it is going to be up to you to get some "dinner" onto the conveyor belt and into the bass' kitchen. This is done with a leadhead jig , usually a bucktail weighing from three to six ounces.

EQUIPMENT FOR JIGGING

Rods

Jigging in the Ditch calls for much heavier equipment than would be used for sight-casting to fish with lures and pencil poppers. Jigging is a completely different animal. Where the more normal fishing can be done with a rod rated up to 4 ounces, the jigging rod is usually rated between 4–8 ounces, sometimes more. You will need a rod that can do several things. One is get you good distance, since distance will matter. At times you will want to cast a hundred plus yards. You will also need power and leverage for fighting big bass and rods rated up to 8 or 10 will do the job for you. Big stripers on the bottom will not just give up and roll up to the surface for you, they will put on a massive battle and there will be times when you as a fisher will have to break the spirit of the fish and winch it off the bottom. The rod has to be capable of doing just that. The other very important consideration is the weight that you will be throwing. You have to have a rod capable of throwing jigs up to six ounces or more. An under-sized rod will break when trying to cast too much weight. You will need to do your homework here. You will find that there are a lot of options and a lot of opinions out there. I suggest you let yourself evolve as a surfcaster. Go to one of the local Canal tackle shops and have a face-to-face with someone in the know about what you want. Buy what you need as you need it. Talk to several different people and get many opinions before you lay out serious dough. It may not be a bad idea to borrow a rod or two to get a feel for a rod that you have heard about or have interest in.

For rod length the standard is between 10 and 11 feet in the majority of situations. As you delve deeper into the Canal fishery you will find that you will need various rods to use for specific techniques in certain situations. One thing that can be confusing about rods is the numbers that are thrown at you. Someone may say to you "oh, that is a Rainshadow 1209." To translate this, the first three numbers are the overall inches of the rod, so in this case, 120 inches, makes this Rainshadow a 10-foot rod (120 inches). The number at the end is the power of the rod. 1 is the lightest, softest action and 9 is the stiffest rod. That makes this Rainshadow a fast-action rod, or a pretty darn stiff rod to put it in layman's terms.

Reels

When it comes to reels for jigging there will again be a lot of back and forth over which one to use, which is best and the age-old argument between spinning versus conventional reels. I have used both and each has certain advantages and disadvantages. I like the precise control that I get with the conventional. The ability to open the bail in an instant is very convenient, and being able to feel your line as it comes off the reel is huge. Conventional also allows you to feel your bucktail as it bounces the bottom, and know immediately that you have a hole and you need to drop it into the hole by opening the bail in an instant. For me the problem (and it's a big problem) has come with the casting distance. I was brought up throwing spin and it is where I am most comfortable. As far as I am concerned spinning allows me monster casts without any fear of "backlash retaliation" from my reel. The last thing that I want to do is pick out a bird's nest at 2 a.m. while I have my optimum tide in front of me. So my suggestion is to go with whatever makes you feel comfortable. The bottom line is that once you are out there and actually fishing, your full concentration needs to be on what your jig is doing, not on other distractions. Do what gets the job done for you!

Your criteria for a reel are important. Jigging is an advanced technique and the technique of jigging puts a lot of stress and wear on the gears. So you need a reel that will hold up to the abuses of this kind of fishing. As I've said before, and especially at this level of the fishing—don't be cheap. Buy good quality.

If you opt for a spinning reel, a longcast spool is an absolute must (see Chapter 2). It will hold a lot more line than the regular-size spool. High capacity is very important for distance casting. The longer shape of the spool also allows line to fall easily off the spool with very little resistance during a cast. Along with that you will want a quick retrieve speed on your reel, a minimum of 40-inches per crank.

Line

Line choice is important. Today the consensus is braided line. Some still use monofilament but I'm not going there. For jigging I would suggest a 40-pound test braid for starters. Opinions differ—some will say 65- or 70-pound test braid, some will say go 30. The advantages of braid over mono are many—small diameter, which is good for casting distance; limpness, which means no memory which is also is very good for casting, and no stretch, which means it is good for sensitivity and you can feel everything when in contact with a fish or the bottom.

When it comes to leader you again have multiple opinions. Being that the bottom of the Canal consists largely of rocks, you will encounter the little monsters at the bottom that eat lead. Getting hung up and losing jigs is very normal—if you are fishing the Canal correctly then you will be in the shop buying bucktails quite a bit. (This is why some fishermen pour their own bucktails.) The problem comes when you need to break off your line intentionally. You want to break it off at the leader, not break your expensive running line of braid. If your braid is 40-pound and your leader is 60, you may have a problem. So common sense dictates that if you are using 50-pound braid, you would use 40-pound leader material or if you are using 40-pound braid then 30-pound leader. That is a very safe approach. Your leader length is safe at between 24–30 inches.

JIGGING THE DITCH

The first thing that you need to do is to find a perch or a spot that will be productive. Finding this spot along will take some serious time investment on your part—great jigging spots are one of the absolute best-kept secrets along the Ditch, and many have taken those secrets to the grave. So you are really going to have to work at this!

One of your main objectives in finding a great spot to fish is finding where one of the "mountains" drops into one of the "valleys." This is where the fish set up during the tides. The next thing, which complicates this process even more, is that you may have to hit certain spots on specific parts of a tide. Some spots only produce on certain tides whether it be a tide direction, east or west, or a certain stage of the tide, for example the hole at Pole XXX is only good on the bottom half of the east tide. Furthermore you may even have specific spots for certain parts of the season, spring, summer, or fall. Eventually you will build what I like to call a spot reservoir, a collection of spots that will you will choose from on specific nights and specific tides. If you catch a fish at one spot, it becomes special, but you must have numerous spots. What if you get to your spot and someone is already there? You go to your next.

Bucktails and Leadheads

Once your scouting is complete now it is time to wet a line. Obviously the purpose of jigging is to be on or near the bottom. You do this by using lead. I am going to reference bucktails in this section because it is the most common to use. The leadhead/rubber combination is the other popular choice.

You are going to need to learn the current speeds of the Canal when you jig because there are various weights that you will need through tidal stages and lunar phases. At slack tide you will need the least amount of weight, since there is no water movement and your bucktail will go straight down to the bottom. As the current increases, so will the weight of your jig.

The sizes of your bucktails will range from two ounces all the way up to six or more. Your weight will be determined by how fast the current is running. On big moon tides you may end up throwing six ounces plus. That kind of weight will wear you out very quickly so one option, instead of continually increasing your weight and getting your butt kicked, is to opt out and perhaps fish the slower part of the tide. On normal tides you should be throwing between three and a half and five ounces, depending upon many factors such as the size of your braid, how hard the water is pulling, or how hard the wind is blowing.

Bucktails come in various shapes, weights, and colors. Having a good variety of weights will help you find the bottom and stay in the strike zone. Also notice how heavy-gauge the hooks are—very important for holding big fish in fast current.

The shape of your bucktail or leadhead may matter. The most common is the bullet head. You will find this on most of the bucktails that you buy in shops. Some favor the cone or pointed head because they descend faster, getting you into the strike zone faster.

Three bucktail styles, each made with a different purpose. (Top to bottom.) The Flathead has a taller profile and swims with a bit more side-to-side action and penetrates nicely. The Arrowhead (made by Stripermaine-iac), was made with a faster sink rate in mind. In deep water, like the Canal, you want a fast sink rate. The Bullethead is the style most common in bucktails today.

The next consideration for your bucktail is going to be color. Does color matter? Well that question there has been discussed and argued since long before we showed up on this planet and it will be argued long after we are gone! There are some soft rules when it comes to color. When bunker or butterfish show up during the day, bone or yellow is common. Wine is a good night color or when squid roll through. Some like dark or black in the dark, others just go with white the majority of the time.

The next detail to address for your bucktail is tail dressing or a trailer. What you put on the tail gives your bucktail profile options.

Since dinosaurs walked earth guys have been using Uncle Josh pork rinds (now no longer available) for dressing, which was actually pig skin. Now the market has shifted to my personal favorite, Otter Tails, which have a shape similar to the pork rinds, but they are made of a soft plastic laminate and have many more sizes and shape options. They work just as well and won't dry out like the pork did if you forgot to put it back into the brine.

When you fish with the rubber/leadhead option, you will find that the weights are different and the rubber will change some things, so you will want to experiment again and come up with sizes and weights that you find useful and efficient.

Casting and Retrieving the Jig

When you cast, you will bounce your bucktail across the top of the mountain and then drop it into the valley where hungry bass may be waiting. Ideally you want to cast right into the valley. You want to cast hard and long upcurrent. If straight out is 12 o'clock, and the water is moving right to left, you will want to cast to around 2 o'clock. Allow your jig to sink to the bottom. You will know that you are on the bottom when the line stops dumping off the reel. You have to feel the bottom! You will know you are on the bottom when you feel your jig bouncing ba-ba-ba-ba-ba-ba-ba. If you are not feeling this Morse code, you need to increase your weight. Too much weight and you will in all likelihood get hung up. If you are too light you will be too high over your strike zone so you have to get your exact weights figured out. You have to be on the bottom! Once it hits bottom, reel up fast to get the rest of the slack out of your line and catch up to the jig, feel it bounce or roll along the bottom, and reel just enough to stay in contact and to keep it from hanging up on the bottom. My goal is always to be a foot or two above the bottom. While the jig sweeps through its range of motion, you want to give the jig a little life. You do this by lifting and dropping your rod, which is literally jigging. A hard, sharp stroke upwards, then let the jig fall back down and then repeat. It is here that you are in the strike zone. Your jig will be in the strike zone for only about 10–15 seconds, depending on how fast the tide is pulling. It is here that it is terribly important to know that your jig is on or near the bottom.

Rob Willis shows how to get it done with bucktails. Here he shows a sweet 48-pound striper. Notice his setup, especially the long cast spool—very useful for jigging where long casts pay huge dividends. (www.johndoble photograhy.com)

At some point your jig will complete its sweep and the line will now come tight to the jig, it will feel a lot heavier and the jig will rise up off the bottom. You are done. It is here that I am going to reel in as fast as I can and get ready for my next cast.

One advanced tip that gives you a little more life in the strike zone, sometimes putting a fish at your feet, is called the "dropback." Once your jig completes is natural swing and begins to rise, you open your bail and drop it back again to the bottom, three to four seconds of drop, that's it. This will give you another extended area of coverage while probing the bottom for giants.

CHAPTER 6

FISHING BAIT IN THE CAPE COD CANAL

Fishing with bait in the Canal is not something that I would suggest to someone just starting out, because there is so much more to learn first, especially the complexities of current, tides, and different bottom structures. Unfortunately many newcomers to the Canal start out fishing bait because they hear about the great action and they want in on it. They are accustomed to baitfishing so they baitfish. But the extremely fast currents can wreak havoc on a bait chucker, due to the rocky bottom that covers most of the Canal. Sinkers get hung up very easily in this environment, followed by multiple break-offs and that leads to frustration.

Now should you even bother fishing the Canal with bait? The answer is a resounding, "Yes!" There are times when bait will be the only ticket in town to putting a bass on your business end. But you will have to be smart and have a good understanding of the tides and the speed of the water on certain tides. Now with that said I will also say that there are many ideas, techniques, and theories about how to fish bait in the Ditch. You will, in the end, need to come up with your own system and the one that works best for you, but I will offer you some options. We will discuss chunking and then we will discuss fishing with eels and some live-lining.

Firefighter Tony Navarro used a freshly caught herring to subdue this 43-pound bass. Bait can be used effectively in the Canal in the right time and place. (www.johndoblephotography.com)

BAIT FISHING WITH CHUNKS

There will be times in the Canal when the fish will turn up their noses to artificials and they will only hit natural baits. There are several baits that are available in the Canal, or pass through at one time or another, that would make good bait for the surfcaster. Some of the top chunk baits would be menhaden/pogies, mackerel, squid, sea herring, and even sea worms. Striped bass will eat just about anything in the sea—bass are about adaptation and eating to survive, they are not terribly fussy. For all the chunking that I have done and for all the big bass I have taken on chunks I must stress this one very important point: Be sure that whatever bait you use, it is fresh! Fresh bait outfishes all other baits hands down. Frozen bait is not really an option in my book. By fresh I mean same-day caught or very close (well preserved). The bait also needs to be well taken care of, well iced and protected until use.

We will discuss two ways to fish chunks in the Canal. One is fishing on the bottom utilizing sinkers, the other is drifting baits in the current.

Equipment for Chunking

For bait fishing you are going to want a rod that is rated much heavier than your plugging stick, it should be rated at 4–8 or 6–10 ounces. You will be casting a lot more weight than you would if you were throwing artificials, six to eight ounces of weight plus a chunk of bait. Note that bait fishing is not an exacting part of the sport and you don't need the equipment that you would if you were throwing artificials. So a 10- to 11-foot rod, a little more on the inexpensive side, would do great. As for a reel the same holds true, buy a good blue-collar reel, but don't cheap out. Load it up with 40–50 pound braid.

Rigs for Chunking

There are a couple different rigs that can be used for chunking. One is a rig that uses an egg sinker. The sinker is attached to the running line by attaching a barrel swivel, then six inches or so length of leader material which will hold the sinker, another barrel swivel, and then your drop of leader to your hook (see illustration). The weight slides a little in between the swivels to give the angler a direct feel to the bait. The principle here is that the egg will roll a bit on the bottom and, based on the way it sits, will minimize snags. The other rig is more conventional, the fish-finder rig. Your running line runs through the fish finder and then attaches to a barrel swivel and then a drop of leader down to your hook. Your sinker is then clipped on to the fish-finder. This allows maximum movement of your running line with nothing to inhibit this movement and the connection to you. You can feel the bait directly and the fish can run a little without feeling the stop until it is (hopefully) too late.

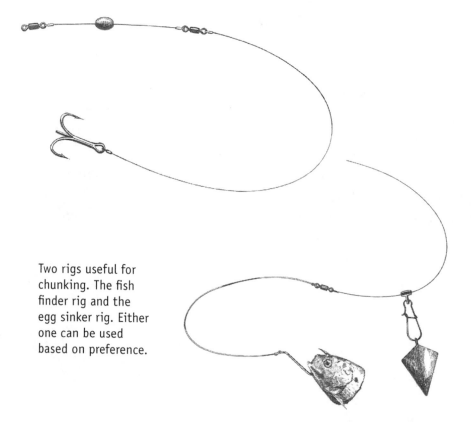

Two rigs useful for chunking. The fish finder rig and the egg sinker rig. Either one can be used based on preference.

Now that you have your two rigs you now have to fill in some details. That would be the size of the leader material that you plan on using, the length of the leader, and the size of the hook. This area all comes down to personal preference, and several other contributing factors that you will need to determine on your own, but I will give you these guidelines. For leader material I would go with 50–60 pound test monofilament. Some may go lighter on the leader that is holding the egg sinker, using maybe 30–40 pound test. That way if the sinker does become lodged, the line can be easily broken without losing a lot of line. For a hook size I would recommend anywhere from a 7/0–10/0 Gamakatsu Octopus hook or Live Bait hook. Circle hooks could also be considered based on personal preference. The hook will largely depend on the size of the bait that you are using. When throwing a larger size chunk or maybe half a bunker or mackerel, I'd go with the 10/0 because I love a wide gap for a fish with a huge mouth. If throwing an average size chunk you may want to use a 7/0–9/0. Again I would also recommend size #2 Spro barrel swivels, and be sure that your fish finder rig is braid friendly or else the braid will cut right through it on the cast.

For leader length, it will again come down to personal preference. There are two important considerations here: one is that a long leader will helicopter in flight and will absolutely kill your casting distance. The shorter you make your leader the more casting distance you will get. Two, a long leader allows for your bait to spin badly in the current and spin equals a big twisted mess. You want your bait to float and flutter in the current, not spin. The bottom line is that you will need a short leader. I would recommend anything from six inches up to maybe 12 at the longest. Again this will end up coming down to your system and to what works best for you. You will need to figure it out as you go.

You may have noticed that I have not mentioned sinker weight—we will cover that under the technique section.

Now before you head out you will want to get a nice new plastic five-gallon bucket to carry all your goodies. Put a couple of stickers on it so you look and feel cool. Be sure you have the following: a sharp knife, a small cutting board, extra tackle (hooks, barrel swivels, fish finders, etc.), leader material, a rag, scissors, bug spray and sinkers. Don't forget your waderbelt. You may also want to carry a rod spike to set your rod in while you wait for Betsy. Bring your flashlight early or late in the day.

Chunking Technique

Ask experienced Canal chunkers what rig to use or the best place to fish and you will get many different answers—but ask them when to fish and the answer will always be the same: slow or slack water. When you have water that pulls as hard as the Canal does you will have a very, very difficult time throwing sinkers and bait into the water and not coming up with either nothing or a huge and ugly tangled mess! Chunking in the Canal has to be done on the slower ends of the tide in order to be effective. A good window would be from 45 minutes before slack until 45 minutes after slack. The moving water will be both your enemy and your friend. While the moving current carries your scent and draws fish from a distance, it also causes you to hang up on the bottom. As the tide still moves at a good pace you will need more weight, perhaps up to six to eight ounces. As it slows you will be able to decrease your weight down to maybe five ounces, as you will still need the weight for casting distance and holding power for your chunk. For the fish-finder rig I suggest you use bank sinkers as they are the most rounded and therefore rock-friendly, if there is such a thing. If you are fishing bait and you cannot hold with eight ounces, go to the nearest Dunkin Donuts and relax for a while.

One of the things that you may want to consider when choosing a spot to fish is the bottom contour—you may want to stay out of the rocks. There are parts of the Canal that have sand-covered bottoms, and if you can find these places you'll save yourself from unwanted frustration. Being that Cape Cod Bay and its surrounding beaches are sand, you shouldn't be surprised that the east end of the Canal sports a lot of sandy bottom and thus is a place you should consider. As a rule anything from the Fish Pier at Scusset Beach and east could offer you good possibilities for chunking.

When chunking any bait, be sure to have a sharp knife and a small cutting board. Cut off the tail and head first, dispose of the tail. The head is the most important piece you have. Next cut out the belly and put it aside, perhaps to use as chum. You then cut the remainder into three to four pieces, perfect for chunking or drifting bait. Remember, don't bury your hook in the bait.

You are going to want to cut a reasonable size chunk for bait. Some guys will throw a half a bunker or mackerel out but for starters I would start a little smaller, maybe a quarter, until you get the hang of it. Cut your bait into four pieces. Don't bury the hook in the chunk, you want to leave a decent portion of the hook exposed so you can get good penetration while setting the hook. Placing a hook anywhere in the back section of a bait is always best as that area is the toughest part of the fish.

Now it is time to cast out. You will have a sinker and a chunk of bait hanging from your rod, well over 10-ounces. To get this out you need to cast with a slow lobbing movement. You do not want to load up the rod and cast fast or hard, because the heavy weight may break the rod. Once your bait hits the water and sinks, reel tight to contact, and be sure you can feel what is going on down below. Wait for the strike. Be patient! You need to let the scent from your bait travel downstream in the current. The fish will then find you. A way to increase your chance of getting a fish is to fish two rods. Cast one out further and keep one closer to shore. I check my bait every 15 minutes, check for tangles and that your bait looks good. Don't hesitate to change your bait often.

Once you have your bait where you want it your next concern will (hopefully) be fighting a fish. You want to keep your drag pretty darn tight (remember big fish and big current). By wrapping your hand around your line and pulling it off the spool, it should be pretty hard to pull off. Wear a glove or some kind of hand protection when doing this with braided line. If you have to pull hard to get it off, you are very close to where you want to be.

Drifting Bait

Another interesting way to fish bait is by drifting your chunks downstream without any weight. This can be done while the tide is moving. You first need to find a point, a part of the canal that sticks out further than the rest. Here the water pulls fast and a lot of fish like to use the rip that comes off the point to set up and wait for bait to get swept into their kitchen, or should I say dining room. It is a great place for drifting chunks. This situation would be perfect for fishing conventional tackle. Open your bail or put the reel in free spool and let the chunk go, pay out line as it goes. Now the trick here, if you are really serious about catching some nice bass, is to chum the rip before you start chunking. You can buy chum or better yet you can mix up your own. My fishing partner and I used a meat grinder to grind up our own bait. You then take it, mix in some saltwater, and you are ready. Bring a bucket and a ladle and occasionally toss some of your raw fish soup into the rip for 15 minutes before you introduce your chunk. The bass will come right up into your rip and you may even be able to hand feed them like you would at the aquarium.

FISHING WITH EELS

Fishing with eels I would generally classify as a more advanced form of surfcasting, and it is no different in the Canal. For those starting out you may want to ease into this technique, build some skill sets first. For those looking to up their game, keep reading! Throwing eels in the Canal is most effectively done at slow or slack water. Sometimes you will throw the eel without any weight and you will let the eel do what it wants to do naturally, swim to the bottom and hide in the rocks. You will want it to swim down but you cannot let it hide or get into the rocks. If you are having a problem keeping the eel down, you may want to throw on a small weight to aid the descent. Adding weight could be as easy as stuffing a ¼ ounce sinker into the eel's mouth before you put the hook through the lips. You could use rubber-core sinkers. You can also do an egg sinker rig using ½- to ¾-ounce egg sinker and then only six to eight inches of 50–60 pound monofilament leader to the hook. The hook size is a personal preference—some like the 5/0 Gamakatsu's Octopus or Live Bait hook, I like mine a little bigger, around 7/0. Remember that the hook will also work as a weight to help get the eel down.

Another option for eels is casting them out to the middle of the Canal, doing so again at slack tide. You want to use a 3–4 ounce egg sinker, using the egg sinker rig previously mentioned. Cast it out as far as you can and then reel it back in, very, very slowly. With this technique you can also fish fresh dead eels with a good result.

Like most striper fishing, eeling and catching big fish should be done under the cover of darkness. It is here, in the dark, quiet, night waters where the big girls relax and put on the feedbag. If you want to have a real good shot at a big fish, fish the two-hour window around slack tide in the dark.

Locations

Finding a place to fish will be your next challenge. Once again you can use points and the rip coming off your point to drift your

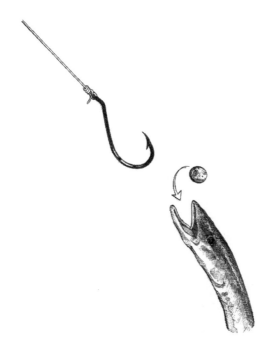

When drifting eels, sliding a splitshot into the eel's mouth before inserting the hook gives you just enough weight to keep the eel down in the current. Too much weight and you hang up on the bottom.

eel down-current to holding fish, much like we discussed in the Drifting Bait section. Another thing to look for is swirls and areas of turbidity, I call it upwelling, where fast current hits a large boulder below and forces water up to the surface. A vertical current of sorts is created. Bass often use these areas to feed and ambush bait. Another consideration when choosing a location to go eeling is to target either end of the Canal—the idea is to hit any bass moving into the Canal as the tide slows and changes. Bridge abutments also make good target areas. These areas offer very deep water and a great piece of structure where hard-pulling currents create conditions that make it hard for bait fish to keep control. It is a magnet for big stripers. Good structure is always a good area to target.

To do eeling right you need to spend some time scouting the Canal and studying certain tides at certain times. Try to scout by day and then execute your plan at night. I carry a notebook for jotting down notes and hunches. In those notes I mention, of course, direction of the tide, and the exact time of the tide that I see something that I think has potential. For example, I find an upwelling and a whirlpool that I think looks great and it is happening approximately two and a half hours after the tide goes east at pole 80 MS (Mainland Side), so I write that down. Or I like what the water does as it slacks on the west tide three poles west of pole 220 CS (Cape Side). Note anything and everything, and build a plan for a certain night and try to fish as many of your scouted places as you can in a logical progression. If a spot has a payoff, you note it. If a spot ends up being a dud, you cross it out. You will end up building a reservoir of spots that you like on very specific tidal stages. The Canal is a huge body of water so I would start with one section of the Canal and master it and then end up learning the entire thing over time. You will end up with a nice list of spots that you will make it a point to fish at very specific times.

Equipment for Eeling

For eeling you are going to want to go with a heavier stick, ten to eleven feet long, one rated in the 4–8 ounce or 6–10 ounce range. You will need this for casting your eel and the weight out as far as you can when necessary. You will also need a stick like this because you will be flirting with big girls that in all likelihood will have some serious attitude problems. If you are just tossing eels with little or no weight, then you can go with a lighter rod.

CHAPTER 7

A BRIEF HISTORY OF THE CAPE COD CANAL

Based on all the happiness that the Canal has brought to thousands and thousands of anglers, it would make you think it was given to us by a God that loves us and wants us happy. So it is hard to believe that it was made by mere mortals—yet the Cape Cod Canal is man-made, and here is a brief history.

Before the Canal two rivers flowed in the area, the Manomet River which flowed southwest into Buzzard's Bay, and the Scusset River which flowed into Cape Cod Bay. An area of about a mile separated the two. Talk in the early days was about how good it would be if the two rivers connected, which would have made trade by boat possible. Such discussions date all the way back to the Plymouth Colony in the 1620s. Fast-forward 150 years and George Washington, thinking it would be advantageous for American ships to have more protection, ordered Thomas Machin, an engineer with the Continental Army, to check into it in 1776. He returned with the recommendation that the Canal be built, which was the first legitimate attempt at a plan for digging the Canal. The plan was never executed, but plans for building a canal surfaced from time to time for over 80 years since Washington's first inclinations.

AN EARLY CANAL

Interestingly enough there was a canal made in 1717 that connected Cape Cod Bay to the Atlantic Ocean at Orleans. It would take a day or more off the sailing trip up and around the outer Cape. Jeremiah's Gutter, as it was called, stayed active for over a hundred years. It fell out of use and was later replaced by the Cape Cod Canal.

SHIPWRECKS

Besides providing a shorter passage to Boston and points north, the Canal was also built to help reduce the number of shipwrecks that were happening on the outer coastlines in places like Martha's Vineyard, Nantucket and the Outer Cape. The path through the Canal would save thousands of ships and lives during treacherous weather. Over a 130-year span before the Canal was built, there were over 3,500 shipwrecks, an average of 26.92 shipwrecks per year or 2.25 shipwrecks per month!

The real work on the Canal got started on June 22, 1909. The project was spearheaded by August Belmont Jr., a wealthy man who showed interest in the Canal project. Belmont purchased the Cape Cod and New York Canal Company, which he reorganized, and then hired a famous civil engineer, William Barclay Parsons, to

The steamer the City of Columbus was a famous wreck that went down off of Martha's Vineyard in January 18, 1884 after hitting the Devil's Bridge reef. The ship left Boston with 45 officers and crew members and 87 passengers, of which only 17 crew and 12 passengers survived. It was wrecks such as this that put emphasis on an inland route to points north, thus the need for the Cape Cod Canal to be built.

develop a detailed plan. After this engineering study was complete Belmont decided to move forward on the project. On June 22, 1909 he ceremoniously shoveled the dirt at Bournedale and promised "not to desert the task until the last shovelful has been dug." Though a noble cause, Belmont was going to use the Canal for profit as any boats passing through it would be paying a toll. The work on the Canal was tougher than expected, as they hit huge boulders that needed to be dynamited for removal, not to mention cold winters which brought work to a halt. Boulders were brought on schooners from Maine to build the huge breakwater on the east end. On the west end two dredges were put to use digging from the Buzzard's Bay approach. By 1910 the project was proceeding at full speed. They dug from both directions with more than 20 dredges in use. At this time the Buzzards Bay Railroad Bridge was completed, 160 feet long and pivoted on the Mainland side with a huge counterweight. The Bourne Bridge was completed on 1911 and the Sagamore Bridge was completed in 1913 and allowed traffic to move freely across the spans. Unfortunately the two car bridges only had a 140-foot opening for ships to pass through. With the Canal's hard-pulling currents, boats at times would have real problems navigating and especially waiting while the bridge was down.

The work was proceeding too slowly, so Belmont hired the American Locomotive Company from Paterson, N.J. to construct two massive dipper dredges at the Canal. One, The Governor Warfield, was set up on the west end and the other, The Governor Herrick, was situated on the east end. By August 1912 the two were working and digging toward each other; the work was progressing and the project was in its final phase.

The dredge Governor Warfield at work.

In April of 1914 the Canal was near completion. Belmont and Parsons shook hands and mixed bottled water, some from Buzzards Bay and some from Cape Cod Bay, with only a dam, nicknamed "Foley's Dike," standing between the two bodies of water. It was removed on July 4, 1914 and the two waters combined. The Canal opened on a limited basis on July 29, 1914, when they had a ceremony and a parade of ships that included steamer *Rose Standish* and the destroyer *McDougall*, along with Belmont's personal 81-foot yacht, *The Scout*. The Canal was officially completed almost two years later on August 10, 1916 but it was not without issues. At this point it was 100-feet wide and 20-feet deep, and took a weird turn at Phinney Harbor on the west end, at Buzzard's Bay. The narrow channel, and the hard-to-negotiate bridges, caused wrecks that hurt the Canal's ability to produce revenue. Although it knocked 62 miles off a ship's trip, it never produced enough money to please the investors. In 1915, 2,689 ships had moved through, 4,634 the next year. Still, Belmont's idea was a financial failure.

The relatively narrow passageways of the early bridges made the Canal dangerous and caused wrecks. This hurt its ability to generate revenue early on.

WHAT'S NEXT?

On July 21, 1918, a German U-boat, *U-156*, surfaced and let loose on the tugboat *Perth Amboy* and its four barges in tow, three miles off of Nauset. This aggravated the top brass so the Director General of the United States Railroad Administration took over the Canal under a Presidential Proclamation from Woodrow Wilson, and ran the Canal until around 1928. In 1928 the government purchased the Canal for use as a free public waterway. It was bought for $11.4 million and $21 million was then spent on improvements between 1935 and 1940. The width was increased to 480-feet and the depth to 32-feet, making it the widest canal of its time. The west end was re-done so there would be direct access from Buzzard's Bay as opposed to running through Phinney's Harbor.

One of the major issues with the Canal up to this point was the bridges, which were a hazard and were causing anxiety in the shipping business. The bridges were usually left in the down position, which is dangerous for ships navigating in fast currents. So the Army Corps of Engineers arranged to build three new bridges, two car bridges and a train bridge. The highway bridges were completed at the same time, in 1935. They spanned around 600-feet across and at center they were 135 feet above the average high water mark, meaning that the Canal would accommodate any sea-faring ship. The railroad bridge was built as a vertical lift bridge, which means the entire bridge rises horizontally and in unison. It stays suspended until a train is coming, then it is lowered. (It is really cool to see.) The railroad bridge opened on December 29, 1935.

The Railroad Bridge was completed in 1935. Here you see the bridge in the down position as a train crosses it. Notice also the lobsterman retrieving his trap.

During World War II ships used the Canal to avoid German U-boats that lurked in the ocean waters beyond. The Canal was protected by a coastal artillery battery at Sagamore Hill Military Reservation, which thankfully never fired. But the danger was quite real. On June 28, 1942, the Mystic Steamship Company's *Stephan R. Jones* hit something it wasn't supposed to and sank in the Canal, closing down the waterway and temporarily forcing all shipping around the outside. Soon after the ship SS *Alexander Macomb* was torpedoed in July 3, taking 10 souls to the bottom with it. The Canal re-opened on July 31 after the *Stephan R. Jones* was dynamited and removed.

CHAPTER 8

CANAL ETIQUETTE

When you get a bunch of obsessed, passionate fishermen together in a relatively tight place catching nice-sized stripers, throw in the fact that probably seventy percent of them don't fully understand what is going on, you then have a recipe for potential disaster.

When you have guys that have fished the Ditch since diapers and then you have newcomers to the fast waters with undeveloped skill sets trying to catch their first bass, and they both have to work in close proximity, you may have some fireworks.

Or when you have a guy who has been fishing for two hours without a bump, who suddenly hooks up and then gets mugged by eight new friends who watched from the road, you run the chance of tempers flaring and people's feelings getting hurt. The word etiquette starts floating around. Etiquette is about respect. I love respect because if there is respect then there can be harmony, without respect there can be ugliness and fisticuffs. Giggle if you want but it can, and has, come to that.

I believe that in surfcasting it comes down to common sense and common sense is giving space, space is respect. Give adequate space to the guy you are going to fish beside. How much is adequate? At the Cape Cod Canal, when fish are on the feed, that's about 15 yards or about 50 feet. That's a respectful distance. Communication is also important—nicely say to the guy that just moved within ten feet of you, "Hey buddy I feel you are a little close, why not moved down a little bit so we don't cross up?" That's polite and good but it may (probably will) not work, but start off being nice. If that does not work then I give them the Muller Hippo Hurricane Holler, which is more on the opposite end of the spectrum and usually loaded up with superlatives and suggestions of where to put things.

Before we go any further I want to mention to the newcomer or first-timer, that if you are new to the Canal situation, and the fishing is going off and there are a lot of fish being caught and things happening very fast, if you don't have the proper-sized equipment or you don't yet have the skill to cast straight out or to fight big bass in fast water, you may have to take a pass and sit and watch and learn. There is very little worse than a poorly skilled angler surrounded by sharp shooters and doing nothing but wreaking havoc. Please have the self-awareness to know it's time to back out. You can always take a walk down the service road to a quieter area, but please use good discretion.

TIME WITH THE KIDS

Taking your kid fishing is highly recommended! I am a strong believer that it is better to go fishing with your kid today than it is to go hunting for him tomorrow. There is no greater joy than watching your son or daughter catch his or her first fish. Lord knows I raised four kids so I know! Now catching the first Canal fish will be a special moment but please let me say this respectfully, taking your kid into a blitz situation when there are people and fish and flying lures all over the place, throw in high emotions, it is probably a better idea to do it away from the mob. When the fishing gets nuts, people do too. Sideways casts and impatient people can make for a terrible first-time experience. A child getting hooked or seeing violence has to be avoided. If you or your kid isn't skilled enough to handle the blitz situation, use good judgment and stand and watch and learn.

RULES OF ETIQUETTE FOR FISHING THE CAPE COD CANAL

I have put together a list of do's and don'ts for fishing the Canal. This is a guide that I developed after talking to some very well respected Canal fishermen who have been doing it for a very long time. Most of the locals at the Canal are very fair and they are good guys and great fishermen but again it comes down to making good decisions. If you are polite I don't think there will be any problems, most of the guys may even help you with some pointers or tips—just remember to be respectful.

- Consider Others First. If everybody shares and works together it could make for an enjoyable experience. Do to others what you would have them do to you!

- First Come, First Served. If a guy has a spot or the spot you want, it's his. Move on. If you don't like it, get to the spot earlier.

- Proper Spacing/Don't Mug Anyone. Give enough space for the next guy to fish and to function without interference from you. If you think you may be too close, you are! If a guy is into a fish, it is not right for you to jump into his spot or to "mug" him. Be smart—be courteous! Watch what direction the fish are moving and move down and get in front of them and wait for the fish to arrive.

- Get Your Fish in Quickly. Once you hook your fish, this is not the place to play your fish with a long drawn-out battle. Put the screws to it and get it in. If you have guys beside you they will wait for you to get your fish in, to a point. If it isn't coming easy, then you may have to walk down stream with the fish, excusing yourself as you go. This is also one of the reasons for the bigger rod, power and control. I also need to mention that this is the reason why you want to be sure your drag is set tight enough so that the fish doesn't run and run and end up in Provincetown.

- Button Your Lip. If you are fishing and a good body of fish comes by and all neighboring rods bend over, don't call in your "goon platoon." It isn't fair to the other guys that have been there to have sixteen guys suddenly show up and crowd out the guys that were there first. Remember the body of fish is moving, think about it. Just fish and enjoy the hit you have!

- Ask In. If you see a spot that you just HAVE to have (you probably don't) and someone is in that space, and if you can't find another spot nearby, it is polite to ask for permission. A quick, "Would you mind if I fished here?" would be the right thing to do. You may get rejected but at least you did it respectfully.

- Time Your Casts. When the ranks get tight, and the water is sweeping hard, it will become obviously important that you have to time your casts as to not cross the guy next to you. Continually crossing your neighbor does not make for longstanding friendships. My rule is simple, when your neighbor casts out wait until he is halfway in on his retrieve, at that point it is safe for you to cast normally and to just do your thing. Do this and you will seldom have problems.

- Take Care of Your Fish. If you love catching stripers think about the future. It is better for our striped bass future to release your fish to fight another day. It is very important to get the fish back into the water as quickly as possible. Remove the hooks quickly and gently toss the fish headfirst into the water. Do not let it roll in the dirt, and try not to touch the body if possible as the slime coat is very important to the health of the bass. Do not drop it. Unhook it, take a quick picture if you want, and then release the fish quickly. Time matters.

- Don't Dump on the Ditch. If you carry it in, carry it out. I think every guy that goes down to the Canal in the morning carries a cup of coffee. What happens to the coffee cup when it is empty? It gets thrown into the rocks. Lunch containers? On the ground. We have been given a beautiful place, please don't dump on it! Take your garbage, your discarded line, everything with you when you leave.

- Watch Where You Are Parking. There are plenty of places to park along the Canal's seven-mile stretch, some of those however are limited to a certain amount of cars or certain hours. We must be respectful of these areas because abuse could very well lead to loss of privilege. Be smart, if you are not sure please go park somewhere else.

THE INTERNET AND SOCIAL MEDIA

While the Internet is useful for gathering information and looking stuff up like tides or weather, it also has its drawbacks, especially when it comes to fishing. Facebook and the like have given people to ability to instantly post photos or information. People read the posts about a blitz somewhere and then decide, "Wow, now may be a good time to go fishing!" Before you know it 73 guys show up at the spot. Like it or not, social media and the internet are here to stay. Gone are the days of secrecy and keeping everything under wraps and close to the vest! There have been times when I have done my best job of keeping things quiet, only to have another less successful angler see me and then post an instant report based on what he sees me do. What the heck is that?! Needless to say, I had to say goodbye to that spot! Facebook has ruined the sanctity of surfcasting.

The internet has also bred a nasty brood of surfcasters that don't work, don't put in their time and have no regard for anyone else's feelings. They more often than not travel in groups or do what I call "fish by committee." They would be lost if they ever had to fish alone. These fishermen, and I use that term loosely, strike fear into the true bloods and the old-school guys that actually put in their time, because in a wink of an eye and a Facebook post, their hotspot can be overtaken by a 12-headed monster that has real bad breath, rods swinging all over, Magic Swimmers flying and cell phones blazing. This kind of behavior is simply wrong and shouldn't happen. There needs to be respect for the guy who has been there, paying his dues.

CONSIDERATION FOR THE FUTURE

I have been fishing for many years and while I haven't seen it all, I have seen a lot. I have seen the bad and I have seen the good. I lived through a moratorium where the striped bass was on the verge of extinction and they had to restrict the keeping of bass. From the mid-70s until 1991, striped bass reproduction was terrible, far below what was considered average. For years we hardly saw any stripers, my "big" surf rod was a seven-foot St. Croix Ben Doerr, which was all I needed for the bass I was catching. For about 10 years or more we feared the worst and we just figured that soon we would all be deer hunting or fishing for pike in Canada. Then out of desperation we started getting smarter, all catch and release, we cleaned up the rivers, started getting rid of dams and creating a healthier striped bass environment. Then they started to make a recovery. The years 1989 and 1993 produced good spawning years well above the average. We started seeing stripers again highlighted by tons of small fish. Then came the mother of all motherloads, the year 1996, the best spawning year ever! The recovery was well on its way and the stocks were finally considered recovered. The small fish turned into big fish. Once again surfcasting happiness ruled supreme and everyone was content.

But when the fishing got good again everybody forgot the lean years! 2011 was the year the '96 class came of age, by that I mean the entire class averaged somewhere in the mid-30 pound range. We caught fish like mad! Nice fish too! But then we started killing recklessly and paying no respect to the fish—everywhere the striper went it was pressured and killed. The Jersey Shore, Long Island, Montauk, the Block Island boats, Rhode Island, the Canal fishermen, the outer Cape—this great fish was pressured every-where it went including Carolina in the winter months, while it staged. The class got no reprieve! It is my opinion that year class (1996) has been eliminated, that gene pool, that spawning group, has been wiped out by unnecessary killing. There isn't an endless supply of striped bass. We all need to be responsible for the future of the striper that we all love so much. If you love catching bass then you have to love releasing them! Catch your fish, and then release your fish. Have your cake and eat it too! Catch it, weigh it, take a couple quick pictures, and release it. What else do you need? If you love being out there and catching stripers, you have to let the supply replenish.

Consider the Future—Yes you have the right to do whatever you want to do with your fish, but if you love being out there and the pull of a good bass then you have to strongly consider releasing your fish!

This is one of the best sights that you can see as a striperman. A big fish that you just battled, being set free to see another day.

INDEX

Tactical Angler, 38

Tail dressing, of bucktails, 81

Terminal tackle, 37

Tide Chart, 19

Tides, in Cape Cod Canal, 18;
    morning, 22

Tin lures, 48

Tsunami Fat Shad, 61

Tsunami shads, 56

U-156, 102

Uncle Josh pork rind, 82

Upwelling, 95

Waderbelt, 43

Waders, 40

Wading boots, 40

Wally's Pencil, 61

Washington, George, 97

Water movement, through
    Canal, 21

Weight, of bucktails, 59

Wilson, Woodrow, 102

World War II, 103

Zooplankton, 27